Muslimah Mumpreneur

Strategies for Muslim Women to Successfully Thrive in Business and Motherhood

SARAH GULFRAZ

Copyright © 2025 Sarah Gulfraz

Sarah Gulfraz has asserted her right to be identified as the author of this Work in accordance with the Copyright, Designs and Patents Act 1988.

All rights reserved.

No portion of this book may be reproduced in any form, stored in a retrieval system, stored in a database, or published/transmitted in any form or by any means, electronic, mechanical, photocopying, recording or otherwise, without prior written permission of the publisher.

Dedication

~ **Bismillah** ~

May Allah (swt) accept our efforts and grant us success in this life and the next. Ameen.

In dedication to my loving family and all their support.

Contents

1. Introduction — 1
2. Understanding the Dual Role of Motherhood and Business — 5
3. Setting Up for Success — 19
4. Building a Support System — 31
5. Integrating Islamic Principles into Business and Motherhood — 39
6. Creating a Productive Work Environment at Home — 50
7. Time Management Techniques for Busy Mothers — 59
8. Self-Care and Personal Well-being — 68
9. Nurturing Relationships and Family Life — 81
10. Leveraging Technology for Efficiency — 91
11. Reflecting and Adjusting Your Balance — 100
12. Conclusion — 111

Find Out More — 114

Chapter One

Introduction

Both men and women are essential and indisputable in all spheres of life, like two wheels of a social machine. If they engage in commercial endeavours, both will contribute to societal economic development. According to the law, women can begin any legitimate business to support themselves.

For this reason, it has been seen as a key component of development in the world's most developed countries. In addition to generating employment, it also boosts the nation's economy. One factor that has been thought to affect entrepreneurial activity is religion. It instructs, permits, and advances the community's system of cultural values.

Women's financial independence is important in Islam for several reasons, such as giving them the freedom to make their own decisions, protecting their independence and dignity, and enhancing the general well-being of the family and community. As a Muslim woman, being able to support your family financially can improve your ability to serve Allah (SWT) and advance society.

Economic fairness, social well-being, and entrepreneurship are all encouraged by the Islamic economic system. There is ample historical evidence that women can conduct business in accordance with Islamic principles. Both men and women are encouraged to work hard and earn legal money by the holy book of the Quran and the Sunnah.

This shows that women are permitted to pursue entrepreneurship, as many of the prophet Muhammad's (PBUH) female companions, known as *sahabiya*, were involved in various business ventures that are permitted in Islam. The prophet himself encouraged women to pursue a variety of endeavours, and trade and commerce were one of them; his own wives were among the most successful traders of that era.

Hazrat Khadija (RA), the first wife of the Prophet Muhammad (PBUH), is a well-known example of a Muslim businesswoman. She was a successful trader in her day, proving that it is acceptable for women to engage in economic ventures. Islam has provided several rules for their day-to-day business dealings. Economic expansion and social advancement are propelled by entrepreneurship. Equal business participation by women promotes economic success and the growth of a more just and balanced society.

In the world of entrepreneurship, the road to success is usually paved with setbacks, disappointments, and uncertain times. However, the path of a Muslimah mumpreneur is characterised by tenacity, faith, and purpose since, in addition to strategy, commercial success necessitates faith, fortitude, and the courage to keep going when everything else seems lost in order to discover Allah's (SWT) blessings.

There is no doubt that for many Muslim women, it's really hard to manage the business with their motherhood and other responsibilities simply. It may seem overwhelming. These responsibilities may include raising children, managing a household, and, most importantly, upholding the values of Islam this can feel like an all-encompassing role, making it difficult and challenging for entrepreneurial aspirations.

According to Islamic customs, all business dealings, including those of entrepreneurs, must aim to fulfil religious objectives. According to Islamic law, a Muslim's primary objective in business must be to please Allah (SWT). This includes working in accordance with the moral and ethical guidelines of Islamic customs, carrying out one's religious duties, and supporting the larger Islamic objective of enhancing society at large.

That's why religion and business are inextricably linked in a fully Islamic entrepreneurial framework. As a result, the set of economic behaviours is governed by secular, legal, and ethical rules and religious rules. A significant component of entrepreneurship in Islam is fulfilling religious duties; as a result, success is evaluated not only on the basis of financial gain but also on ethical considerations, which, in accordance with Islam, may earn the entrepreneur benefits in the afterlife.

Entrepreneurship can alter a nation's economic issues. It also attracts a large number of employees and independent contractors and is a means of earning a legitimate living. Making a legal (halal) living is not just a financial endeavour in Islam; it is also a religious duty that is firmly ingrained in one's beliefs.

The importance of halal income is emphasised in the Quran and Hadith, which connect it to social welfare, moral behaviour, and heavenly favour. Just engaging in legal activities—avoid those that are forbidden in Islam, like interest-based transactions, gambling, or the sale of haram goods—while maintaining moral and honest business practices is all that is required to generate a halal income through a business.

The world of business has changed dramatically now. It offers endless opportunities for men as well as for women to contribute meaningfully and also provides space for females to manage their families while doing business. However, there are a number of reasons why Muslim women may avoid doing business, the most significant of which are social, cultural, and psychological.

Since they are frequently the only carers, they could also have trouble juggling job and personal obligations, which makes it challenging to dedicate time to launching and operating a business. Nevertheless, every issue has a solution. This book aims to give you useful skills and knowledge that will enable you to meet the obstacles and seize the chances that come with being a Muslimah mumpreneur.

At the heart of this book is the concept that success is not about choosing between motherhood and business but about integrating both into a fulfilling and harmonious life. As a Muslim female, your primary task is to redefine success on your own terms, align your work with your values, and use your skills and talents to make a positive impact.

As a Muslim woman in business, you are obliged to start with strong intentions and put your reliance only on Allah (SWT). This guide will act as your companion on this journey. Each section of this book will offer practical advice, real-life examples, and actionable steps to help you build a successful business while being a devoted mother. You will understand the power of learning and integrating Islamic principles into your work life for your overall well-being.

This book is here to empower you and make you realise that you are capable, worthy, and equipped to create a life of balance, success, and fulfilment. So, take a deep breath, set your intentions, and start your journey with confidence. The world needs your talents, your voice, and your contribution. Your journey starts now.

Let's dive in!

Chapter Two

Understanding the Dual Role of Motherhood and Business

The Modern Muslim Woman's Role

Dual obligations in life may be a special and ever-changing struggle, especially when juggling the demands of parenthood and business. This delicate act calls for a harmonic interaction between two seemingly demanding worlds beyond simple time management. Mothers who own their businesses must constantly balance their obligations to their children with their business needs.

Finding a sustainable balance begins with acknowledging that your family and business require substantial attention. The emotional complexity is genuine, such as the worry experienced when a work conference interferes with family time or the guilt experienced when a business opportunity is lost due to a child's performance. These emotions are normal and a part of the process. However, when handled purposefully and with assistance, this very balancing act can bring to light the fortitude, resiliency, and flexibility present in both roles.

Balancing Traditional Roles with Contemporary Expectations

Women play a variety of significant roles in the family as mothers and wives, but today's women and their lives have changed significantly as a result of modernisation. Women have also been able to advance and actively participate in the growth of their countries thanks to increased access to education, jobs, and socioeconomic change. Because of this, the majority of women today play two roles and balance their personal and professional lives. It is essential to strike a balance between traditional duties and modern expectations because any imbalance could have negative effects on one's personal or professional life.

Prior to the arrival of Islam, women were frequently expected to stay within the family setting and be submissive mothers and spouses. Men were expected to protect and provide for their families. With the arrival of Islam, women could have positions as academics, leaders, and even military advisors.

Islam encouraged women to seek knowledge and contribute to their societies by granting them the rights to education, property ownership, financial independence, and social involvement. Islam also promoted women's participation in trade and business as a means of advancing society. Islam acknowledged that women have the same rights as men to own property, own businesses, and participate in economic pursuits.

Islam has improved the status of women in various areas, including social, political, and economic rights. It advocates for women's empowerment and rights. The fact that Muslim women were granted rights 1400 years ago shows that the monotheistic faith has enabled women to take charge of their own lives and claim their rights.

Hence, Muslim women continued to exercise essential societal roles for centuries—managing households, raising children, and even running businesses. But nowadays, due to modern-era needs, the challenge lies in maintaining harmony among the obligations while meeting the demands of a rapidly evolving world. Islam has given rights and freedom to women but also bound them to stay within the boundaries of Islamic teachings.

Operating a business often conflicts with the conventional expectations of mums as primary caregivers and homemakers, necessitating a careful balancing act between personal obligations and professional goals. Women who want to establish a successful career and lead satisfying family lives must understand this dual responsibility. So, for many Muslim women, the goal should not be to abandon tradition but to integrate it with modern opportunities.

The Evolving Role of Muslim Women in the Business World

> *"And that man shall have nothing but what he strives for" (Quran 53:39)*

Work and action form the foundation of the world. According to this directive, Allah (SWT) provided all His creatures with tools to capitalise on their strengths and protect themselves from harm. Humans—being the most complex—have greater needs and responsibilities, requiring more effort to sustain themselves, support their families, and contribute to society. Since Islam is a natural and social religion, everyone must work to support themselves, meet societal needs, and improve the lives of others. From an Islamic perspective, both commerce and labour are essential and valued components of a righteous life.

The roots of the Islamic concept of entrepreneurship can be found in the Quranic verses that support it, as Allah (SWT) stated:

> "...to men is allotted what they earn, and to women what they earn. But ask Allah of His bounty, for Allah has full knowledge of all things" (Quran 4:32)

> "...On earth will be your dwelling place and your means of livelihood for a time" (Quran 2:36)

These verses highlight the importance of working and earning Halal income.

> "Nobody has ever eaten a better meal than that which one has earned by working with one's own hands. The Prophet of Allah, Daoud, used to eat from the earnings of his manual labour." (Sahih Bukhari)

According to the Quran and the Sunnah, it has its own entrepreneurship culture and tenets. In Islam, women are also permitted to work and own their enterprises. Islamic history shows that many Muslim women were successful in education, business, and medicine. Women were involved in trading even during the time of the Prophet Muhammad (PBUH), who encouraged them to pursue business.

The Prophet Muhammad's (PBUH) first wife, Khadijah bint Khuwaylid (RA), was a well-known and successful Makkah entrepreneur. She is a role model for Muslim women entrepreneurs in her era. In her community, she was a highly respected and knowledgeable woman. She gave the Prophet (PBUH) emotional support and encouragement, which greatly aided in the propagation of Islam. Amazingly, she was also a devoted wife and a loving mother to six children.

Khadijah (RA)'s commercial ventures began with her father, Khuwaylid (RA), who was considered one of his tribe's most powerful members and worked hard to conduct commerce throughout the Arabian Peninsula and its surrounding nations.

With the help of her husband, Abu Hala, a very successful businessman, Hazrat Khadijah (RA) walked in the footsteps of her father and became an entrepreneur. She gave him all the support he needed to succeed in the company, but he passed away a few years later. She began learning wealth management strategies from this experience, and as a result of these experiences and her inheritance of riches, Hazrat Khadijah (RA) became a potential merchant who could handle her resources sensibly and autonomously.

Many prominent female traders existed during the time of the Prophet Muhammad (PBUH), including Umm al-Munzir binti Qays and Asmah binti Makhzemah bin Jandal. Additionally, during the reign of Saidina Omar, a female trader named Al-Shifa binti Muawiz was chosen to serve as the Medinah market's "commandant." Khaula, Lakhmia, Thaqafia, and Bint Makhramah were among the other ladies who dealt in oriental oil-based fragrances. These examples clearly illustrate that the Prophet's (PBUH) female companions engaged in business.

Similarly, agriculture was mostly carried out by the women of Al-Ansar in the fertile rural areas surrounding Al-Madina. The Prophet's (PBUH) companion, Sahl Ibn Sa'd, told of a woman who owned her own property. After Friday prayer, she would grow barley and beets to feed the Prophet's (PBUH) companions.

Asma' (RA), the daughter of Abu Bakr (RA), stated that she and Zubair were not wealthy when they married. About two miles from their home, the Prophet (PBUH) granted them a piece of land. She personally cultivated the crops and delivered them. According to Asma' bint Abu Bakr, "I was returning one day with date stones on my head. Then, along with a few residents of Madinah, I met the Prophet (PBUH). I was asked to ride on his camel's back with him. It was clear that women were involved in farming; they also carried agricultural products. Instead of carrying items on their heads, Asma (RA) and other women would have used modern trucks, railroads, ships, etc.

Therefore, Muslim women have the right to work, own property, enter legal agreements, and manage their assets as they choose. They have always been a part of economic and entrepreneurial landscapes. Today, Muslim women entrepreneurs are utilising their skills and talents across various industries, from e-commerce to education and technology.

The rise of technology and digital platforms has made it easier for individuals to launch businesses from home, enabling them to effectively balance their professional goals with family responsibilities. With access to global markets, networking opportunities, and flexible working models, more Muslim women are thriving in business without compromising their Islamic values.

Defining Success in Both Areas

The majority of successful people believe that establishing a prosperous profession or managing a business requires full-time dedication. Nonetheless, many women in the business sector today are doing their best to balance their families and careers. Being a mother is a wonderful and rewarding experience, but it takes time and effort, particularly during the first few years. History refutes the stereotype that women who become mothers are incapable of juggling a fulfilling profession and a family. In addition to parenting their children with love and care, women can also accomplish amazing things in their careers. Let's have a look at how!

What Does Success Look Like in Motherhood and Business?

Success in both motherhood and business for a woman is deeply personal, and it always varies from one woman to another. As the nature of each person is different from one another, for a few women, success is considered as financial independence and career fulfilment, while for the rest, it may be more important to nurture a strong faith-driven family. True success is not about achieving a perfect balance; the real goal is finding a rhythm that aligns with one's priorities and values.

Motherhood doesn't have to be sacrificed for a successful career. Being a CEO and a supermom simultaneously, often at the same hour, can make it challenging to manage; ensuring that none of the balls falls hard enough to shatter is more important than simply keeping them all in the air. Perhaps building a multimillion-dollar business empire isn't the key to your success.

It all comes down to earning enough money to provide a decent living for your family. Ensuring every dollar counts and aligning every business decision with your personal values are just two of the challenges that come with this practical goal. The key to success is figuring out what suits your situation and making deliberate decisions that support both roles.

In Islam, success revolves around one's faith, character, and contribution to the well-being of others.

> *"And those who believe and do righteous good deeds, they are dwellers of Paradise, they will dwell therein forever." (Quran 2:82)*

This verse highlights that ultimate success is tied to what is right and the pursuit of goodness in all spheres of life, including motherhood and business.

> *"And do not consume one another's wealth unjustly or send it [in bribery] to the rulers in order that [they might aid] you [to] consume a portion of the wealth of the people in sin, while you know [it is unlawful]." (Quran 2:188)*

This verse encourages business owners to be fair, transparent, and just. Thus, a Muslim woman is free to start a business and can excel while upholding her faith and values.

Setting Realistic and Achievable Goals

There is never enough time to do everything that has to be done. As a mother and businesswoman, you're always searching for methods to increase your daily productivity, frequently at the expense of your own sleep. Finding methods to become more efficient is beneficial and necessary for your sanity because of the unrelenting pace. It's a wild ride. One moment, you're ecstatic over a business victory, and the next, you're grappling with guilt.

When pursuing entrepreneurial goals, many mothers experience the typical emotion of guilt. Don't allow guilt to prevent you from reaching your objectives. Remember that following your passions and building a life you love provides a great example for your children. You're demonstrating to your children that anything is achievable with courage, perseverance, and hard work. Maintaining the health and happiness of your heart is essential to succeed in your business and your family. You're the lifeblood of both.

Pursuing major ambitions as a busy mother with life's continual demands and pressures can feel tough. But in reality, the way to fulfil the needs of a busy mother is to set goals. Setting realistic goals that align with one's ability is crucial for success in motherhood and business. Despite concentrating on a single objective, divide it into more achievable steps or milestones. As a busy mother, this strategy lets you balance other obligations while making consistent progress. Instead of striving for perfection, create little goals because high expectations can cause stress and dissatisfaction.

For instance, instead of trying to work long hours every day, as a mumpreneur, you can set aside dedicated business hours that fit within your family's schedule. Be realistic about how much time you can commit to achieving your goals. Consider your daily routine, your responsibilities to your family, and other commitments. Set deadlines that will motivate you without causing unnecessary stress or compromising quality.

Similarly, defining success in motherhood might mean being fully present during key moments, such as mealtime or bedtime, rather than being available 24/7. The key is to create a system that accommodates both professional and personal priorities.

Challenges and Opportunities

Common Challenges Faced by Muslim Women Juggling Both Roles

The psychological, social, cultural, economic, structural, and other obstacles are only a few of the numerous obstacles that prevent Muslim women from becoming entrepreneurs. Compared to their male counterparts, female entrepreneurs who are mums are more likely to be in charge of childcare, homeschooling, and household duties. This greatly affects their health, stress levels, and productivity.

Juggling multiple responsibilities and a divided focus often makes Muslim mothers feel overwhelmed. Efforts to manage business activities, household duties, and fulfilling personal commitments often lead to exhaustion. Without a structured plan, it can be difficult to allocate time effectively, leading to stress and inefficiency.

Entrepreneurs face innumerable obstacles as they manage a business. These difficulties range from monetary difficulties to emotionally taxing roadblocks. But if we focus on the mumpreneur community, we notice that their challenges reveal another level of complexity. Mumpreneurs frequently struggle to balance the complex business demands with their responsibilities as mothers.

Managing the roles of a mother and an entrepreneur gives them a dual duty that demands excellence on all fronts. Their journey involves more than just making their business successful; it involves balancing the deep obligations of raising a family and pursuing entrepreneurial pursuits. This complex balancing act requires a degree of resourcefulness and perseverance that goes beyond the typical difficulties experienced by entrepreneurs.

During the early stages, there is a lot of parenting and business management going on simultaneously. After the children leave for university, a different kind of busyness with a lot of worries appears. This results in a stage of life where people wonder, "Will everything eventually be fine?"

Success in the context of mumpreneurship is a multifaceted accomplishment that reflects both commercial victories and the capacity to provide a loving home environment. These women are trailblazers not only in entrepreneurship but also in changing how society views work-life balance. Their story embodies the willpower, creativity, and steadfast attitude needed to succeed in two positions that are both demanding and enlightening.

The strain of juggling their business goals with their family obligations is one of the biggest obstacles female entrepreneurs face. Women are typically expected to be the primary carers in many communities, whether for children, ageing parents, or other family members.

The time and emotional commitment required for this caregiving job can be substantial, leaving little time for the energy needed to operate a profitable business. Many female entrepreneurs are put in a position where they must be excellent at both being a carer and an entrepreneur. They may find it difficult to devote themselves entirely to their business endeavours due to the significant anxiety and stress that this dual obligation can cause.

There were a lot of time management issues while juggling the demands of a new company with childcare obligations. Despite numerous attempts to create guidelines for better time management, it was still difficult to manage both areas efficiently.

Family support frequently plays a crucial role in the success or failure of female entrepreneurs in patriarchal settings. Women's business ventures may be viewed as secondary or even superfluous in situations where traditional gender stereotypes assign males as the main breadwinners and women as the carers.

However, women frequently depend significantly on their families for logistical, financial, and emotional support to successfully shift from the home to enterprise. Without this support, women might be compelled to lower their goals, impeding their ability to grow and succeed in their enterprises.

This dynamic is particularly noticeable in rural or less urbanised areas, where traditional family duties are still more rigid. Support can come in many different forms, such as providing childcare, financial assistance, or even assistance with the company's day-to-day management. A woman entrepreneur's ability to succeed or fail can be greatly impacted by this type of family support. The unfortunate truth is that many women lack this network of support, making their entrepreneurial path even more difficult.

Mumpreneurs suffered emotionally from balancing their jobs as mothers and business owners. Taking care of their kids while juggling the responsibilities of their jobs became emotionally draining. Furthermore, they frequently struggled with guilt about putting work obligations before family time.

One of the most valuable resources for any entrepreneur is time, but for women, managing time is made more difficult by psychological and social norms. Women are frequently expected to provide most of the care in various communities. In addition to taking up a lot of their time, this social expectation creates a psychological barrier that makes them doubt themselves and reduces their desire to take risks in their business.

Furthermore, women may have a mindset that undervalues their skills or even rules out entrepreneurship as a feasible option due to societal expectations. Many cultures expect women to take care of the home and prioritise the well-being of the family, leaving the commercial world to males. Women may, therefore, be reluctant to take chances or go for business prospects out of concern about social rejection or failure. Women may be reluctant to take the risky actions required to expand and scale their businesses as a result of this anxiety, which can keep them from giving their all to their enterprises.

It can be challenging for female entrepreneurs to balance their carers and business owners' responsibilities. They could feel bad about not spending enough time on their enterprises when they spend time with their families. On the other hand, they could feel guilty about not spending enough time with their families when they concentrate on their business. Women may experience psychological exhaustion as a result of this internal conflict, believing that despite their best efforts in both areas, they are never really succeeding in either.

Imposter syndrome, a situation in which people believe they are not worthy of their accomplishments or that they will be revealed as frauds, is another way psychological obstacles appear. Because of the pressure to play many roles, women are more likely to suffer from this illness, especially in patriarchal countries. These psychological obstacles can keep women from taking the chances required to launch a profitable company, especially when paired with the outside pressure of living up to social norms.

As a result, launching a new company presented unique difficulties. Many mumpreneurs were managing their first business endeavour, which included managing vendors, hiring qualified staff, and handling marketing and financial matters. For others, obstacles were interface, customer acquisition, and awareness.

For many female entrepreneurs, juggling business duties with personal and family obligations is a major drawback. Women frequently take on disproportionate caregiving and home responsibilities, making it difficult to dedicate time and effort to their enterprises. Burnout, stress, and possible compromises in their personal or professional lives might result from this work-life imbalance.

Thus, balancing business and motherhood while staying connected to one's faith can be challenging; a packed schedule may leave little time for personal reflection, worship, and self-care, which are essential for long-term success and fulfilment.

Identifying Opportunities for Growth and Fulfillment

By using a variety of tactics and getting help, mumpreneurs can overcome their obstacles. These are:

Many of us suffer from a scarcity mindset during these uncertain economic times, which is based on a fear of scarcity and the belief that we must compete for few resources. The transition from a scarcity perspective to an abundance mindset creates opportunities for cooperation, acknowledging others' accomplishments, optimism, creativity, innovation, problem-solving, limitless possibilities, and increased corporate success.

Take part in personal development activities that ease emotional stress and increase self-confidence. This could entail participating in programs to boost confidence, practising positive affirmations, and asking mentors for assistance. Attending a self-confidence session could benefit mumpreneurs who battle self-doubt while juggling their obligations to their families and businesses. She can feel more capable and empowered if she learns how to get over impostor syndrome.

Women are socialised to prioritise others before one, so we frequently fail to ask for the assistance we require. This can make many entrepreneurs feel even more alone and isolated, so figuring out how to get more assistance is critical. You are unstoppable as a business owner when you are operating in accordance with your goal and are surrounded by like-minded others.

To avoid burnout, take pauses and rest. Make time for enjoyable and restorative activities, even if they are brief. Overall well-being and productivity may increase as a result. People who manage both work and family obligations can plan little pauses during the day to read a book, go for a walk, or practise mindfulness. These little recharges can increase your energy and sharpen your attention.

Poor time, energy, and resource boundaries are common problems for female entrepreneurs, which can result in burnout, tiredness, and business failure. By accepting that it's acceptable to have difficult times, you can cultivate self-compassion. To reduce emotional stress, participate in self-care practices like journaling, meditation, or spending time with loved ones. A mumpreneur who feels guilty about losing family time due to job obligations should try practising self-compassion. She can find emotional comfort by recognising her efforts and permitting herself to take care of herself.

Pursuing work-life balance, managing time strategically, and navigating emotional complexities are characteristics of the mumpreneur's journey. Problems like time management, emotional strain, and work-life balance highlight the particular demands these extraordinary women face. Nevertheless, a set of tools for empowerment and uplift is used to confront these issues head-on.

Challenges often come with valuable lessons. Instead of viewing obstacles as setbacks, they can be seen as opportunities for growth. Every challenge provides a chance to refine strategies, reassess priorities, and strengthen personally and professionally. Muslim mumpreneurs can build resilience and achieve long-term success by continuously learning and adapting.

The journey of a Muslim mumpreneur is one of purpose, perseverance, and fulfilment. While the path may be demanding, it is also deeply rewarding. By embracing both roles with confidence and faith, a woman can create a meaningful and successful life that aligns with her values, aspirations, and family commitments.

Chapter Three

Setting Up for Success

Success for mumpreneurs in both their business and family life aspects does not happen by chance; it requires efforts and hard work for intentional planning, discipline, and a deep commitment to balancing priorities. According to Islamic principles, navigating these responsibilities depends on a structured approach that effectively aligns personal values with entrepreneurial ambitions. Now, let's explore how to create a unified vision for your family and business, set clear priorities, and manage time effectively to ensure success in both areas of life.

Creating a Family and Business Vision

As a Muslim mumpreneur, balancing faith, family, and business often demands a clear and intentional vision. The peaceful journey requires both your family and business to complement each other rather than compete for your attention and energy. What you need on an initial basis is that you, as a mother and businesswoman, must redefine the term success according to the requirements that align with your own life, not just financially but spiritually, emotionally, and socially. Never consider what this success means for others. Always pay attention to that side, what it means for you, and what you require to achieve it smoothly.

It's not something you can copy by seeing how others deal with it because each person's journey is unique and different, so start by asking yourself. What type of changes do I need to achieve this success? What kind of home environment do I want to create? What are my expectations of raising my children? What values do I want my business to reflect? By finding the solutions to these questions, you can craft a vision that aligns with your Islamic principles and personal aspirations.

A well-defined vision provides direction. Highs, lows, and erratic, wild curves are all part of family life. It's hardly surprising that families can occasionally veer off course. But if we don't have a clear vision, we may find ourselves in circumstances and locations we didn't want to be in. Vision for mumprenuers not only helps them to prioritise tasks, make better decisions, and stay focused on long-term goals but also provides them with the framework and how to gauge their progress as a parent.

Without a clear vision, you may find yourself tangled in the difficulties of this journey, failing to meet the demands of your business while feeling disconnected from your family. As Muslims, we believe that intention (niyyah) is the foundation of everything. Intention is essential in establishing the moral worth and outcome of any deed.

> *"Actions are but by intention, and every man shall have only that which he intended" (Sahih Bukhari)*

So, before embarking on your entrepreneurial journey, set an intention to have a vision of a business that goes beyond your financial gain. Your business can serve others, contribute to your community, and earn sadaqah jariyah (continuous charity) by providing halal products or services.

Having a strong vision doesn't mean not facing difficulties; it means preparing yourself by having a clear purpose and staying strong in tough times by navigating obstacles with resilience. Always trust in Allah's (SWT) plan and seek his blessings.

> *"And seek, through that which Allah has given you, the home of the Hereafter; but do not forget your share of the world. And do good as Allah has done good to you. And do not desire corruption in the land. Indeed, Allah does not like corrupters." (Quran 28:77)*

While striving for business success, never neglect your duties towards your family or compromise Islamic values. Stay committed to your values, and remember that both motherhood and entrepreneurship are powerful ways to contribute positively to the world.

Aligning Personal, Family, and Business Goals

For mothers, goal-setting is essential because it gives purpose and direction. It enables you to concentrate on the most important things to you and your family. Establishing clear goals can help you prioritise your work, make wiser decisions, and efficiently manage your time. Setting and achieving goals gives you a sense of success and motivates you. Aim propels you ahead as an entrepreneur, yet having too high of an aim can cause frustration and fatigue. Instead, set attainable goals that are in line with your priorities.

The most important thing is to have a plan. As working mothers, we need to take action to support our own goals and spend more time with our children. Successful goal-setting for mumpreneurs necessitates deliberate work. It's not a simple task. As a result, coming up with a plan is crucial. If you're more successful at setting goals, you'll immediately have more time and be able to prioritise your path to achievement.

Among other things, poor goal-setting affects your self-worth, time management, and determination. Any ability you possess has the potential to become a successful business if you put your mind to it. To begin with, most of us are terrible goal-setters. In just a few weeks, we generate original ideas, become enthusiastic about one, and then forget about it. Because of this, establishing goals enables us to see our goals and develop plans of action to assist us in reaching them.

Set short-term objectives first. For example, aim for a 10% increase in monthly sales rather than doubling your company's income in six months. This will encourage you to keep going by making it seem achievable. Long-term objectives are just as significant. Make sure your objectives align with your values, whether that means enjoying a family vacation or growing your business. If things don't always go as planned, don't be too hard on yourself and instead celebrate your victories, no matter how minor.

Set S.M.A.R.T goals. "S" stands for time-bound and specific. Provide answers to crucial questions such as who is involved, what you hope to achieve, where you plan to do it, why, and by when. "M" stands for measurable; it entails having a checklist of actions to accomplish your goals and ensuring they're reasonable. The amount of money you need to invest and whether it fits your present budget are two realistic factors to consider.

"A" is achievable or reachable. Possess the necessary mindset and skills to achieve your stated objectives. When creating goals, it's crucial to ask yourself these questions. Is this the person I want to be when I grow up? Is this me? Do your objectives match who you want to be in the future? "R" is for reasonable. Given that it requires your time, goals ought to be reasonable. Be truthful about how much time and effort you'll devote to your business. You should be sufficiently challenged by your goals to be inspired. "T" is on time. Have a deadline, and keep pushing.

You can set S.M.A.R.T. objectives for the daily tasks that will make you more productive and less overwhelmed once you have mastered setting S.M.A.R.T. goals for larger things.

By aligning your family and business goals, create a roadmap that ensures your efforts are cohesive and meaningful. A strategic roadmap tracks progress along the route to help guide decisions, including the key actions and benchmarks needed to achieve a desired state. By providing a visual guide that links strategy and execution, it maximises resources and gives the task direction.

The strategic roadmap ensures alignment and guides the execution process by breaking down those goals into manageable steps. The strategic roadmap is your visual path to accomplishing business outcomes through completing deliverables related to those outcomes. Make use of it to deconstruct strategic goals into feasible projects and deadlines.

Developing a Clear Vision for Both Areas of Your Life

Increasing your motivation or willpower won't make you healthier, fit, or more purposeful as a mother. It all comes down to having a clear FOCUS, committing to achieving your goals and defining SMART goals connected to your fundamental beliefs. It involves streamlining your life, scheduling the important tasks, and eliminating the things that divert you from your goals. Your effectiveness will increase with your level of attention, regardless of what you hope to accomplish in life. This also applies to mumpreneurs.

A well-defined vision serves as a compass that navigates your path and provides direction to your daily decisions and long-term strategies. If, as a mother, you decide to run a business, then make sure that the activities of your business do not pull you away from your family. It should be easy to manage your role as a mother and a wife. If your business creates hardships to manage your personal life as a mother, then your whole family can get disturbed. You must try to set clear intentions for each role you play to help you stay focused on what is important.

For example, if one of your family goals is to have more quality time together, then activities relevant to your business should be structured in a way that allows flexibility. If your business goal is financial stability, then defining a sustainable work schedule that does not compromise family life is crucial. Writing down your vision in a tangible form, such as a vision board or a journal, can make your aspirations feel more concrete. Reflect on it regularly to ensure you are on the right path and make adjustments as needed.

Establishing Priorities and Boundaries

Although the idea of work-life balance may seem unattainable, achieving harmony between your personal and professional obligations is feasible. But only if you employ the appropriate techniques. The goal of work-life balance is to establish a long-lasting balance between your personal and professional obligations. This balance is essential for sustaining mental health, building family ties, and guaranteeing economic success for parents who are also entrepreneurs.

In simple words if you want to live a more grounded life and become more centred, you must make the mental and emotional space necessary for it. It's difficult for mothers to prioritise themselves and express their needs and desires in a clear and confident manner. But if you're struggling to find the much-needed work/life balance, now is the moment to take action. Making time and space for grounded centredness is the first step towards achieving balance.

Establishing boundaries entails separating work and personal time and letting your family know when you must prioritise your business. Making a schedule that helps you stay organised and on course can also be beneficial. Setting reasonable goals and developing the ability to decline assignments that conflict with your schedule or ideals is critical. Making time for yourself and putting self-care first is equally crucial since it will help you avoid burnout and enable you to give your utmost in both your personal and professional life. Recall that establishing boundaries is essential to preserving a positive work-life balance and is not selfish.

The fact that limits are personal is the most crucial thing to keep in mind. It's okay if your limits don't look the same as other people's. You must take the time to define them according to your own preferences. Think for a moment: What do you need to do for your company? What are your partner and family in need of? What do you require to feel balanced and supported? The secret is to experiment with various boundaries, evaluate how they feel, and make any required adjustments.

Remember that boundaries exist to support you in living and working according to your principles and goals. By identifying, owning, and adjusting them, you can create a life that nurtures both your business and personal well-being.

Techniques for Setting Priorities Effectively

The amount of work required to create a profitable and successful business might be overwhelming. It's crucial to understand, though, that your work as an entrepreneur is not your top priority. Your home and how you care for it are your first priorities as a mother. And by keeping it in mind, we may maintain the proper order of our priorities.

Since you and your spouse are the heads of your household, the home also includes your marriage. Motherhood is the most important thing after taking care of your marriage. Raising your children properly to provide for and nurture them is necessary, and that takes your attention and time.

Managing can be difficult, but prioritisation makes it easy. Balance is essential. Begin by distinguishing between urgent and important tasks. Not everything that demands your attention is truly essential.

Although our to-do lists as mumpreneurs may seem endless, not every item on our lists is equally crucial. Identify your top priorities in your family life and company by taking a step back. Which duties are necessary to advance your business? Which pursuits make you and your family happy and fulfilled? Don't be scared to assign or let go of things that aren't helping you; instead, concentrate your time and attention on these priorities.

A practical approach is to categorise your tasks into four groups. First, target the "urgent and important" tasks which require immediate action, such as attending to a sick child or responding to a time-sensitive business issue. Second, consider "important but not urgent" tasks, including long-term plans, such as business growth strategies or homeschooling schedules.

Thirdly, pay attention to "urgent but not important" tasks. These seem pressing but can be delegated, such as answering non-essential emails. And lastly, do not forget about "neither urgent nor important." These activities can be minimised, such as excessive social media scrolling. Identifying what truly matters helps you invest your energy in activities that contribute to your overall success and well-being.

Time Management Strategies

Time is extremely important. The value of time has been explicitly declared by Allah Almighty (SWT) in the Quran. To strengthen our faith in this life and the next, we should manage our time well.

> *"There are two blessings which many people lose: (They are) health and free time for doing good" (Sahih Bukhari)*

Thus, as a mother and businesswoman, time is your most valuable resource and managing it effectively will determine how well you balance your dual responsibilities.

Setting a value on minutes and hours results in profitable returns on your time, much like when you budget every dollar in your personal and professional life; time cannot be made, but money can! In a day, everyone has the same amount of time. The way each individual chooses to spend that time is the sole distinction.

Start each day with a strategy aligning with your life's goals, values, and to-do list. Set aside specific times for self-care, family activities, and work-related chores. Planning regularly enables you to actively engage in a future where you may be present and contribute from a place of plenty rather than tiredness.

Tools and Techniques for Effective Time Management

Busy mumpreneurs like you may accomplish more work in less time by practising time management. It enables you to successfully balance your work and home obligations. If you're ever feeling confused by how little you know about time management, some helpful tools and techniques below can help you:

Wake up early:

The five daily prayers framework is one of Islam's best time management strategies. The ideal way to begin a fruitful day is with the early morning Prayer Fajr. In accordance with the Prophet Muhammad's (PBUH) Sunnah, rising for Fajr establishes a spiritual and fruitful tone for the remainder of the day. When you get up early, you have more time for uninterrupted, concentrated work. The interval following Fajr is regarded as a time of blessings or barakah.

Avoid the urge to return to sleep after Fajr. Plan your day, perform dhikr, or read aloud from a few chapters of the Quran during this peaceful period. This establishes a constructive and upbeat tone for the remainder of your day. Before the daily grind starts, you can spend the hour after Fajr working on a personal project, working out at home, or making a nutritious meal for your family.

Time Blocking:

One time management technique is time blocking, which entails planning every aspect of your day. When you divide your workweek into manageable chunks, you may more easily concentrate on finishing tasks. Time blocking is allocating particular time slots to complete particular tasks.

When you block out your weekly agenda, you can see what's consuming your time. If you're devoting too much or too little time to particular chores, you can make changes to balance things out. You can save time by using this strategy to arrange related tasks together. It enables you to concentrate on the tasks, giving you more time to spend with your loved ones and engage in your favourite activities.

When you employ time blocking, you can see how you spend your time. It indicates your priorities based on the amount of time you devote to each one. Allocating time blocks to more crucial tasks can assist you in making adjustments. You'll be better able to prioritise the truly important things and boost productivity when you're more conscious of how you're spending your time.

Time blocking necessitates thorough preparation. Time blocking compels you to devote time to the things important when planning your week. Setting aside time each week to work on your objectives will help you achieve them if you're prone to setting but not completing them.

Set Task Priorities Using the Islamic Idea of Ihsan (Excellence):

Whether worshipping Allah (SWT) or doing a basic home task, the Islamic concept of Ihsan inspires us to aim for perfection in all we do. Setting priorities using Ihsan enables you to prioritise quality over quantity. You're more likely to finish chores effectively rather than quickly when you concentrate on executing them perfectly. This guarantees you're making the most of the time and effort you put into every assignment.

Decide which three to five high-priority jobs need your undivided attention and effort at the beginning of the day. Start by tackling these, giving them your whole attention and intention, and understanding that your efforts are being made for Allah's (SWT) benefit. Take the time to carefully do your housework with Ihsan rather than hurrying through it. Essentially, make your labour an act of worship. The task's purpose can turn routine tasks into spiritually enlightening endeavours.

Make Use of Technology's Power:

We're mostly distracted by technology, but we can also block those distractions. Apps like Trello, Todoist, and Forest (a Pomodoro timer that also stops you from using other apps once it's set) help you stay focused, organised and productive throughout the day. Next time you're tempted to check your messages or browse social media, you'll remember that you need to finish the task first by using tools that isolate you from distractions.

Use A Calendar for Everything:

Regardless of your chosen tool or method, ensure everything is scheduled. This might mean that Google Calendar will become your new best buddy. By placing everything on your calendar, you can determine whether you're adding more chores than your timeline can manage or setting reasonable daily goals. This can greatly assist you in determining the appropriate priorities for your day.

Additionally, it is unnecessary to specify what should or should not be included, including meals, physical activity, academics, work-related duties, housework, hobbies, prayer, adhkar, reciting times for Quran, meetings, and/or deadlines. The rule is to put whatever must be done on the calendar, set deadlines, and work accordingly!

Islamic time management focuses on making every minute matter with purpose, faith, and intention rather than just finishing things. By planning your day, you can build a balanced existence that supports your business, your family, and your beliefs.

Keep in mind that time is one of Allah's (SWT) greatest gifts and that by making good use of it, you can both perform your earthly obligations and grow closer to Him. Consistency is key. By following a structured plan, you can make the most of your time without feeling stretched too thin.

Success is not about doing everything perfectly but making intentional choices that bring you closer to your vision. As a Muslimah mumpreneur, your ability to create harmony between these roles will inspire others to navigate a similar path.

Chapter Four

Building a Support System

A thriving business and a fulfilling motherhood journey require more than just passion and hard work—they demand a strong support system. For a Muslimah mumpreneur, balancing these roles means knowing when to seek help, building relationships that foster growth, and integrating personal and professional support structures into everyday life. A well-established support system alleviates stress and empowers you to achieve your goals while staying true to your values and responsibilities.

Leveraging Family Support

Islamic society is built on the foundation of the family, and Prophet Muhammad (PBUH) gave great weight to upholding close family relations. He vigorously pushed the notion that fostering a loving and encouraging home environment is crucial for one's spiritual and personal health.

> The Prophet (PBUH) said: "The best of you is he who is best to his family, and I am the best among you to my family" (Tirmidhi)

Therefore, a Muslim woman's family is the foundation of her life, and their support can greatly impact her capacity to manage her house and succeed in business. Giving others intentional verbal and nonverbal expressions of concern, compassion, and affection is moral or emotional support.

When women receive emotional support, their stress levels can be lowered, and they can feel reassured, appreciated, cared for, accepted, and important. Family moral support, on the other hand, manifests family members' compassion, love, and concern. Moral support like this is crucial in promoting wholesome relationships and giving mothers and businesswomen a sense of importance. Additionally, emotional support is necessary to cope with daily stresses and obstacles, such as tension, rejection, and disappointment.

The most important factors influencing women's success as mumpreneurs appear to be internal motivation, social connections, and family support. Women's virtue in managing their own businesses and family support are positively correlated, particularly when the work meets their requirements.

Family members are often the most dependable sources of moral support since they inspire and motivate people to take action in spite of social and cultural constraints.

Engaging Family Members in Your Business and Motherhood Roles

A successful business does not have to be built alone. Involving family members in your entrepreneurial journey can transform your venture into a shared mission, fostering unity and alleviating the burden of responsibilities. By working together, family members contribute to the business's growth and strengthen their relationships through shared goals and values.

A supportive spouse can be a crucial asset in business. They can act as financial advisors, brainstorming partners, or active day-to-day operations contributors. The Prophet Muhammad (PBUH) set a profound example of a balanced partnership with his wives. His first wife, Khadijah bint Khuwaylid (RA), was a successful businesswoman who managed trade while supporting her husband's spiritual and personal growth.

She played a pivotal role in their household and business, demonstrating that entrepreneurship and family life can coexist harmoniously.

The Quran emphasises mutual support between spouses: "They are clothing for you, and you are clothing for them" (Quran 2:187)

This verse highlights the importance of spouses complementing and protecting each other, which extends to supporting their business aspirations and responsibilities as parents.

Children can also play an essential role in family businesses. Depending on their age, they can assist with tasks such as organising, packaging, or even providing creative ideas. Including children in the business instils values of responsibility, teamwork, and diligence from an early age. It also strengthens their bond with their parents and teaches them the significance of financial independence and ethical entrepreneurship.

The Prophet (PBUH) himself involved children in responsibilities and allowed them to learn through participation. Anas ibn Malik (RA) was entrusted with tasks in the Prophet's household from a young age, which helped him grow in wisdom and character. By engaging children in business, parents create an environment where learning extends beyond academics into real-world applications.

Overcoming the Guilt of Balancing Business and Motherhood

Many mothers struggle with guilt when balancing business and parenting, fearing their entrepreneurial commitments may take away from their children's upbringing. However, Islam teaches that providing for one's family is a form of worship.

> *The Prophet (PBUH) said: "It is sufficient sin for a man to neglect those under his care." (Sunan Abu Dawood)*

This hadith applies equally to women who strive to ensure their families' well-being through lawful means. A mother who pursues a business while maintaining a nurturing home sets an example of resilience, hard work, and ambition for her children.

> *Additionally, the Prophet (PBUH) emphasised the reward for caring for one's family: "When a man spends on his family seeking reward from Allah, it will be recorded as a charity for him" (Sahih al-Bukhari)*

The same applies to mothers who contribute financially while maintaining a loving household.

Engaging family members in business is not only practical but also beneficial for personal growth and unity. A supportive spouse, involved children, and a balanced approach to responsibilities contribute to both business success and a harmonious family life. Through faith and a positive mindset, women can fulfil their roles as entrepreneurs and mothers, setting a strong example for the next generation while seeking the blessings of Allah (SWT).

Communicating with Your Family About Your Needs

The foundation of strong relationships is communication. We express our ideas, emotions, and sense of connection to one another through communication. An atmosphere of mutual respect, trust, and understanding is fostered when family members are free to freely express their ideas and emotions. A family's emotional ties are strengthened through candid and open conversation. When family members feel understood and heard, they are more likely to share their thoughts and feelings. This openness fosters deeper feelings of affection, making it easier to support each other during challenging times.

Your family relationships can change if you create an environment where everyone can express themselves freely and respectfully. Effective communication strengthens ties and promotes understanding, whether by discussing difficulties, sharing everyday experiences, or just having light-hearted talks. Ensuring every family member's voice is heard requires listening as much as speaking.

In a family, good communication is the glue that keeps everything together. Understanding one another's emotions, ideas, and viewpoints is more important than sharing knowledge. A happy, healthy family life depends on an environment of trust and respect fostered by effective communication. Think about communication as reciprocal. Listening is just as important as speaking.

Emotional well-being is enhanced when one can express emotions without worrying about criticism or retaliation. Effective communicators are more inclined to talk about their concerns and fears, which helps lower stress and create a nurturing atmosphere at home. This transparency improves everyone's mental health.

Communicating your demands to your family requires honesty and clarity. Instead of assuming they understand, spend some time explaining your difficulties and how they can support you. Regular family check-ins are a great way to make sure everyone is on trhe same page—use them to talk about timetables, impending business commitments, and shared tasks.

Expressing your needs does not mean demanding help; it is about fostering a cooperative environment. Encouraging open discussions where each family member can voice concerns and suggestions strengthens your household's teamwork. With the right communication, your family becomes a support system and an active contributor to your success.

Finding Professional Support

Beyond family, professional assistance can help you manage your business more efficiently, allowing you to focus on growth and quality time with your family. Overcome obstacles to the continued expansion of your business by identifying them. You may now take better action and alter your direction by investing in new knowledge and skills to better understand your business. Additionally, you're not alone in this; you can overcome this uncertainty with professional support. Let's look at how you can find this support.

Building a Network of Mentors and Advisors

No matter how skilled you are, guidance from those who have walked the path before you is invaluable. Seeking mentorship from successful Muslim women entrepreneurs, business coaches, or even community elders who understand the challenges of balancing work and family can provide crucial insights and direction. A mentor can offer strategies for business growth, solutions to obstacles, and motivation during tough times.

Conversely, advisors can include financial consultants, legal experts, or marketing professionals who assist with the technical aspects of running a business. Establishing relationships with such professionals helps ensure your business decisions are well-informed and strategic.

Utilising Professional Services (e.g., Childcare, VAs)

Outsourcing tasks is not a sign of weakness but a strategy for efficiency. Hiring a virtual assistant for administrative work, social media management, or customer service can free up valuable time, allowing you to focus on core business operations. Many successful entrepreneurs use virtual assistants to manage emails, schedule appointments, and even handle content creation.

For mothers with young children, professional childcare services—whether a daycare centre, a babysitter, or a trusted relative—can provide the necessary relief to focus on work without distractions. Islam encourages seeking ease in permissible ways, and delegating tasks when needed ensures that both business and family responsibilities are managed effectively.

Joining Supportive Communities

A strong support system extends beyond family and professional help—it includes a network of like-minded women who understand your journey and offer encouragement.

Connecting with Other Muslim Women in Similar Situations

The challenges of a Muslimah mumpreneur are unique, making it essential to connect with other women who share the same experiences. Online forums, business groups, and local networking events provide opportunities to learn from others, share struggles, and find solutions together. Whether it's a WhatsApp group, a Facebook community, or a local gathering, surrounding yourself with women who uplift and inspire you can make all the difference.

Sisterhood in business fosters collaboration over competition. Instead of seeing others as rivals, Muslim women entrepreneurs can work together, exchange skills, and create business opportunities that benefit everyone involved. Being part of a community where your values and struggles are understood ensures you never feel alone on this journey.

Benefits of Participating in Support Groups and Networks

Support groups provide emotional encouragement, practical advice, and motivation to keep going. Engaging in business mastermind groups, Islamic parenting circles, or entrepreneurship meetups allows you to gain fresh perspectives, stay updated on industry trends, and find solutions to challenges you may not have considered.

Having a strong support network also boosts accountability. When you share your business goals with others, you become more committed to achieving them. Likewise, hearing success stories from fellow mumpreneurs reinforces the belief that it is possible to excel in both business and motherhood.

Building a support system is not about dependence—it's about creating an ecosystem that enables you to thrive. By leveraging family support, seeking professional assistance, and joining communities of like-minded women, you ensure that your business and motherhood roles don't come at the cost of your well-being. You're not meant to do it all alone. With the right support, you can navigate this journey with confidence, strength, and success.

Chapter Five

Integrating Islamic Principles into Business and Motherhood

The journey of a Muslim woman navigating both business and motherhood is one of immense responsibility, challenge, and reward. A strong foundation built on Islamic principles provides clarity and guidance in balancing these roles. By applying Islamic ethics in business, following the teachings of the Quran and Hadith in parenting, and maintaining a deep spiritual connection, a Muslimah mumpreneur can thrive in both domains with confidence and purpose.

Applying Islamic Values to Business

The quest for profits can occasionally override ethical considerations in the fast-paced, frequently competitive world of business and entrepreneurship. Nonetheless, in Islamic culture, morals and ethics are important to all facets of life, including business.

Shariah, the Islamic legal and social structure, serves as the framework for the ethical system in Islam. Islam holds that anything that promotes the well-being of a person or society is ethically right, and anything that harms people is morally wrong. Its ethical code is the cornerstone of an Islamic civilisation and is forever divine. Islamic ethics advise its adherents to fervently guard their actions, words, thoughts, and intentions and to adhere to specific standards and moral codes in their private and public lives, as well as in their business dealings, social affairs, family affairs, and interactions with friends, neighbours, and family.

The Islamic ethical framework is distinctive in encompassing every aspect of human existence. Islam also offers a unique ethical framework for economic interactions founded on values. According to Islamic jurisprudence (fiqh), precise rules guiding business ethics are mostly determined by the concepts of halal (lawful or authorised) and haram (unlawful or prohibited).

Incorporating Ethics and Values from Islam into Your Business Practices

The cornerstones of Islamic business ethics are honesty (Sidq) and reliability (Amanah). Numerous texts in the Quran and Hadith highlight these attributes, stressing the significance of keeping one's word and being honest in all dealings. Muslim business owners are urged to interact with partners, clients, and staff truthfully. A Muslim entrepreneur must uphold honesty in all dealings, ensuring transactions are free from deceit and exploitation.

> *The Prophet Muhammad (PBUH) emphasised the importance of honesty in trade, stating, "The truthful and trustworthy merchant will be with the prophets, the truthful, and the martyrs" (Tirmidhi)*

One key aspect of Islamic business ethics is avoiding riba (interest) and engaging only in halal transactions. Ensuring that products or services align with Islamic teachings fosters trust and earns the blessings of

Allah (SWT). Transparency, fairness in pricing, and fulfilling contracts are essential aspects of conducting business in accordance with Islam.

Investment in companies that benefit society is encouraged by Islam. This entails staying away from industries like gambling, alcohol, and unethical business. Pay attention to halal initiatives that support moral behaviour. Consider business endeavours in healthcare, education, or halal cuisine.

Making a reasonable profit via moral methods is encouraged. This implies no dishonesty or exploitation. Companies should ensure that all parties—workers and clients—are treated fairly. Respect your team and set reasonable prices.

In commercial transactions, Islamic ethics encourage justice (Qist) and fairness (Adl). This entails treating each stakeholder fairly and ensuring no one is the victim of exploitative or unfair activities. Managing a company in accordance with Islamic principles requires paying fair wages, having clear contracts, and treating suppliers and employees fairly.

Islamic ethics strongly emphasise companies' social responsibilities. Entrepreneurs are encouraged to develop goods and services that benefit the environment and society. Sustainability, ethical labour standards, and community involvement are essential to meet this obligation.

In addition, business owners should practice ihsan (excellence) in their work. Whether providing customer service, leading a team, or managing finances, doing so with sincerity and dedication reflects the true essence of Islamic work ethics.

Balancing Profit Motives with Islamic Principles

In Islam, wealth is a means, not an end. The pursuit of profit should not come at the expense of ethical values. A successful Muslimah business owner ensures that financial gain does not lead to greed or exploitation. Instead, she maintains a balance by integrating generosity and social responsibility into her business model.

One way to achieve this balance is through zakat and sadaqah. Giving a portion of one's earnings to those in need purifies wealth and increases barakah (blessings). A businesswoman may also contribute by supporting community initiatives, providing fair wages to employees, and ensuring ethical sourcing of products. A thriving business built on sincerity and ethical values benefits the owner and serves as a form of dawah, showcasing the beauty of Islam through one's actions and dealings.

Islamic Guidelines for Parenting

As a parent, you spend your days tending to your children's needs, running the home, and attempting to find personal time. Even if raising children is still your top priority, you might eventually wish to broaden your professional horizons, particularly if you sacrificed a successful job to raise them. Being a mumpreneur could be ideal if you have an entrepreneurial drive and wish to launch your own company while still having the freedom to be present for your children.

Parenting Principles Derived from the Quran and Hadith

When a child is born, they are fresh to the world and unsure what to do. They are pure by nature, but this purity needs to be cultivated. Leading, guiding, and caring for them falls on their parents. Depending on who they meet and how they interact with others, the child may go either way if left alone. They'll likely continue to act morally and virtuously if their parents take their duty to raise them on al-fitr and to obey Allah (SWT) and His Messenger seriously.

Young children are still developing their sense of right and wrong, as well as appropriate behaviour in their surroundings. For the child to continue doing what is right and pure, it is the parent's duty to teach them how to accomplish this—how to choose their surroundings and the kind of people to be around.

> *"Everyone of you is a guardian and is responsible for his charges. The ruler who has authority over people is a guardian and is responsible for them; a man is a guardian of his family and is responsible for them; a woman is a guardian of her husband's house and children and is responsible for them; a slave is a guardian of his master's property and is responsible for it; so all of you are guardians and are responsible for your charges."*
> (Sahih Bukhari)

Motherhood is one of the highest honours bestowed upon women in Islam. Mothers are frequently their children's first instructors, teaching them religious and important life lessons. Mothers can teach their children the fundamentals of Islam from a young age by educating them about faith, akhlaq (excellent manners), adab (etiquette), and tarbiyah (living in a holistic way of life). A mother's impact is strong and enduring; it moulds her children's personalities and worldviews.

The process of fostering and advancing a person's moral, ethical, and spiritual qualities is known as tarbiyah. It emphasises religious knowledge and real-world application in everyday life and fully encompasses progress. For our children to grow up to be informed, well-rounded, confident in themselves, and certain of their identity and Muslim paths, it is imperative that we, as Muslim women, raise them with tarbiyah.

Understanding the idea of *Tawheed*, or the conviction that Allah (SWT) is completely one, is the first step towards *Tarbiyah*. All other facets of *Tarbiyah* centre on *Tawheed*, the foundation of faith. Noble character qualities like kindness, compassion, patience, honesty, and humility are what *Tarbiyah* seeks to foster. These qualities are necessary for both effective interpersonal relationships and personal development. *Arbiyah* means learning about Islam and putting it into practice regularly. It involves putting the teachings of the Quran and Sunnah into practice; it is not just theoretical.

The Prophet Muhammad (PBUH) said, "Paradise lies at the feet of your mother" (Ibn Majah). A mother's role extends beyond providing for a child's physical needs; she is also responsible for nurturing their spiritual, emotional, and intellectual growth.

Leading by example is crucial. Children absorb more from what they see than from what they are told. A mother who prays regularly, speaks truthfully and treats others with respect naturally instils these habits in her children.

Incorporating Islamic Teachings into Daily Parenting

Incorporating Islamic principles into daily parenting takes deliberate work, but the results may be immensely satisfying. We can put our children on the path to righteousness and *taqwa* (God-consciousness) by establishing a loving, Islamic environment at home, fostering *iman*, and teaching strong moral values.

Islamic education greatly influences children's outlook and character. Educating young people about Islam also helps them develop a sense of self, purpose, and moral principles. As parents, we have an obligation to ensure our children have a solid foundation in Islamic education. This gives our children the knowledge and comprehension of right and wrong as they grow into young adults.

The first step in integrating Islamic education into your child's upbringing is comprehending Islamic ideals and concepts. It's crucial to get acquainted with the teachings of the Quran and our Prophet Muhammad's (PBUH) Seerah. By developing a greater grasp of these values and ideas, you can better convey them to your child and emphasise their significance in day-to-day life.

Integrating Islamic teachings into daily life doesn't have to be complex. Naturally, children imitate their parents' actions and look up to them. Teaching Islamic beliefs through your own behaviour is the first and most efficient method. Your children must witness you live your faith in a genuine way if you want them to grow up with a strong faith. Here's how to accomplish that:

Show your children that you offer prayer (Salah) daily. They'll see that prayer is a significant and regular part of your everyday routine, even if they are too little to comprehend it. Recite the Quran in front of them regularly. Your reading of the Quran will become ingrained in their daily lives, and they'll begin to connect it with family life.

Include Islamic expressions in everyday speech, such as Alhamdulillah (All praise is for Allah SWT), Insha'Allah (God willing), and Subhan'Allah (Glory be to Allah SWT). This will normalise the language of faith. If Islamic behaviour is modelled for children, they will internalise these principles as a component of their own identity. Simple actions like these can create a strong spiritual foundation.

It's also essential to nurture a love for the Quran and Sunnah. Reading stories of the prophets, engaging children in Islamic discussions, and incorporating Islamic values into playtime help reinforce their faith from a young age. As part of your nightly routine, make it a habit to share a brief tale from the Quran or the life of the Prophet Muhammad (PBUH). Adapt the stories to your child's age and comprehension level. Stories such as Prophet Ibrahim's persistent faith or Prophet Nuh's patience, for instance, can impart important lessons about perseverance and faith in Allah (SWT).

Have a conversation with your child after you've told them a story. Ask them what they've discovered or how they believe the prophet felt in a particular circumstance. This will foster empathy and critical thinking, improving their comprehension of the narrative. Encouraging acts of kindness, such as helping others and generosity, aligns with the Islamic principle of serving humanity. Another essential component of Islamic parenting is kindness.

> *The Prophet Muhammad (PBUH) said, "There is no kindness in a thing, but it adds to its beauty, and there is no harshness in a thing, but it mars it" (Sahih Muslim)*

When we treat our children with kindness, we create a safe and loving atmosphere for them. Kindness is dealing with problems with empathy and understanding, especially while establishing limits or correcting behaviour. It doesn't imply laxity or a lack of discipline. It all comes down to treating our children with respect and acknowledging their inherent worth, which teaches them to respect others.

Discipline in Islam is based on wisdom and mercy. The Prophet Muhammad (PBUH) was known for his gentle yet firm approach to correcting behaviour. Setting boundaries with love and explaining the reasons behind rules help children develop a sense of responsibility while feeling secure in their mother's care.

Prophet Muhammad (PBUH) stressed the value of patience in the journey of parenthood, which is full of highs and lows. Patience is more than simply overcoming challenging times; it's also about keeping a steady, composed attitude that comforts and mentors our kids.

Throughout his life, the Prophet (PBUH) showed great patience, especially when interacting with young people. He never rushed them or reprimanded them severely. Rather, he took the time to listen, clarify, and make a polite correction. Patience is an essential component of good parenting. It demonstrates to our children that they are valuable and that we are committed to their development.

In our everyday lives, exercising patience might mean pausing before responding to a child's mistake or taking the time to explain why a particular behaviour is inappropriate. Real change and progress take time, so staying present and fully engaged in our children's education is essential.

Maintaining Spiritual Balance

The significance of manners and etiquette is interwoven with strands of deep understanding, compassion, and respect in the fabric of Islamic teachings. These lessons help youngsters grow morally and socially, setting the groundwork for a life filled with empathy, humility, and kindness. Instilling spiritual values and Islamic etiquette in our children's hearts during the hectic process of growing up becomes a religious duty that not only moulds their character but also promotes harmony in the larger community.

Teaching youngsters about faith (Iman) entails presenting the fundamental tenets of Islam in an approachable and entertaining way. Explain that Allah (SWT) is the sole God who created everything, starting with believing in Him. Explain that angels are Allah's (SWT) unique servants who obey His directives.

Acknowledge that each child learns in a unique way. Adapt your strategy to their developmental stages, learning preferences, and interests. While some kids might do better with hands-on activities and visual aids, others prefer reading or hearing stories. Thanks to flexible teaching strategies, every youngster can interact with Islamic knowledge in a way that speaks to them.

Encourage them to go beyond the fundamentals and cultivate a lifetime passion for studying Islam. Make age-appropriate literature, internet resources, and Islamic educational initiatives available. Encourage their interest and help them learn more about Islamic ethics, history, and current affairs.

Using these techniques, you can establish a constructive and stimulating atmosphere where kids can study and develop their knowledge of Islam. By using Islamic values as a guide, this method helps children better understand their faith and equips them to deal with contemporary world challenges.

Integrating Worship into Your Daily Routine

Amidst the responsibilities of business and parenting, maintaining a spiritual connection with Allah (SWT) is vital. Prayer (salah) constantly reminds us of our purpose and helps us stay grounded. Even with a packed schedule, setting aside time for salah and ensuring it is performed with focus can bring immense peace and clarity.

There are guidelines for praying, and you must gradually educate your children on the fiqh of salah. Simply begin with the fundamental guidelines and gradually add additional ones as they manage the earlier stages. Show empathy for them and teach them with tolerance and understanding, taking into account their age. Pay closer attention to those we are praying for. What reason do we pray to Allah (SWT)? What does praying to Him give you? Teach your children about the benefits of salah and how it affects our lives.

Allowing a child to lead salah, recite the adhan, help set up prayer mats and clothing, or gather everyone together for prayer in jamaat are all beautiful ways to inspire them. For greater rewards, invite your children to pray with you or perform your salah in front of them and encourage them to join you. You may even find it beneficial to prioritise praying some of your salah with your child.

Modern teaching techniques combined with gentle, loving instruction should be used to educate children to pray as early as feasible and gradually. Islam is a kind faith. The teachings of our Prophet (PBUH) were compassionate and loving. This is something we should never forget when instructing our own children. Remain calm as much as possible, don't push things, and remember that they are only kids.

Making dhikr (remembrance of Allah SWT) part of daily tasks—whether cooking, managing business affairs, or tending to children—keeps the heart connected to Allah (SWT). Short invocations like *SubhanAllah*, *Alhamdulillah*, and *AllahuAkbar* uplift the soul and invite barakah into all that we do.

Finding Spiritual Fulfillment Amidst Busy Schedules

As the journey of a Muslim woman in business and motherhood unfolds, it's vital to recognise the lasting impact of integrating Islamic values into daily life. The goal is to succeed financially and leave a meaningful legacy grounded in faith, ethics, and social responsibility. By fostering a mindset of continuous growth, resilience, and spiritual consciousness, the next generation of Muslimah entrepreneurs can thrive while upholding their religious principles.

One of the key elements of fostering strong Muslimah entrepreneurs is mentorship. Experienced women in business should extend guidance to those just starting. Building networks where knowledge, resources, and support are exchanged ensures that aspiring businesswomen navigate challenges effectively while staying committed to Islamic ethics. The Prophet Muhammad (PBUH) encouraged seeking knowledge, and in the realm of entrepreneurship, this means learning from others' successes and mistakes.

Another crucial aspect is adaptability. The business world constantly evolves, and Muslim women must be prepared to innovate while adhering to Islamic guidelines. Understanding modern business strategies, leveraging technology, and continuously refining skills enable sustainability in competitive markets. While striving for success, it's essential to maintain *tawakkul* (trust in Allah SWT) and believe that sustenance comes from Him alone.

Empowering future generations begins at home. Mothers who embody integrity, hard work, and faith inspire their children to pursue purposeful careers. Instilling strong Islamic values in young minds fosters a community of ethical entrepreneurs dedicated to uplifting society. As Muslim women balance faith, business, and family, they pave the way for a future where success is not only measured by financial gain but also by the positive influence left on the world. True success lies in a business that flourishes both in this life and the Hereafter.

Chapter Six

Creating a Productive Work Environment at Home

In today's fast-paced world, many Muslimah entrepreneurs are embracing the opportunity to work from home while managing their families. Once you've decided to become an entrepreneur, setting up your workspace is a crucial stage in this process. When you're just starting, you probably don't want to pay for an office.

However, striking a balance between business and motherhood requires intentional effort. A well-designed workspace, effective work practices, and strategies to manage distractions can transform a home-based business into a thriving enterprise. By creating a productive work environment, a Muslimah mumpreneur can honour her roles both as a mother and a businesswoman while staying aligned with her Islamic values. Let's have a look at how!

Designing a Functional Workspace

Working from home can help women combine their personal and professional obligations, especially for those who are responsible for providing care. Being physically present at the workplace is not necessary when working remotely. Experts can operate from anywhere as long as there is an internet connection.

Women trying to resume their occupations after a long absence can benefit from this type of arrangement. Mothers may work and care for their children simultaneously, making it the ideal option. Additionally, women gain from working from home since they can take advantage of the new employment prospects. In addition to employment opportunities, women can launch their businesses.

Setting up a Dedicated Workspace to Enhance Productivity

A home-based business needs a dedicated workspace that fosters focus and efficiency. Having a separate workspace has several advantages. It provides a space dedicated to work, which lessens distractions and facilitates concentration. Keeping your personal and professional lives apart also helps. When you enter a workspace, your mind immediately switches to work mode. This facilitates the flow of your thoughts and work. Additionally, it establishes a physical border that instructs your brain to concentrate solely on tasks. It also promotes routine and discipline. You can develop a routine that keeps you engaged by working in the same spot. You can establish a routine where you begin working at a specific time of day.

Additionally, having a distinct workstation also helps you stay organised. With everything in reach, you save time and work efficiently. Distractions, procrastination, and decreased productivity may occur without a dedicated workspace. It can also become harder to switch off during breaks or after hours, increasing the risk of burnout and stress.

Therefore, having a distinct workspace is crucial. This will keep various aspects of your life apart and help you be more productive. Savour the benefits of having a dedicated area, such as enhanced concentration, increased productivity, and better work-life balance.

Examine the available space by analysing rooms or locations, considering privacy and noise levels, and creating a dedicated office at home that increases your productivity. Making the most of your surroundings can help you create a productive office that meets your needs and keeps you motivated and focused.

You can also choose a quiet corner of the house that minimises interruptions. If possible, select a room with a door to separate work from household activities. If you have limited space, a well-organised nook or desk in the living room or bedroom can serve as a functional workspace. Investing in a comfortable chair, a sturdy desk, and good lighting can enhance productivity. Natural light is ideal as it boosts mood and energy, while a clutter-free setup encourages focus.

Personalising the workspace with inspiring quotes from the Quran, family pictures, or a vision board can reinforce motivation. Additionally, keeping essential work items within reach, such as a planner, notepad, and necessary technology, ensures efficiency. The goal is to create an environment that signals 'work mode' whenever you step into it, making it easier to transition into a productive mindset.

Balancing Work and Home Life within the Same Space

One of the greatest challenges of working from home is the constant presence of family responsibilities. The temptation to tackle household chores or attend to children's needs can disrupt work schedules. Achieving balance requires establishing clear boundaries between work and home life.

Setting a structured daily routine can help maintain this balance. Defining specific work hours and communicating them to family members ensures uninterrupted time for business activities. For example, early morning hours before the household wakes up or designated nap times for young children can be utilised for focused work.

Additionally, incorporating short breaks throughout the day can enhance productivity. A well-planned break allows time to check on children, perform household tasks, or engage in prayer, helping maintain spiritual and family commitments without sacrificing business goals. The key is to establish a rhythm that accommodates both professional and personal responsibilities harmoniously.

Implementing Effective Work Practices

Managing work-from-home issues and attempting to strike a balance between work and family life are crucial for working mothers. Let's examine a few of my preferred techniques to assist you in mastering this juggling routine.

Time-Blocking and Productivity Techniques Tailored for Home-Based Businesses

If there is one thing to say about the modern workplace, it is that your schedule will dominate you if you don't take control of it. We are aware of how difficult it is to strike a balance between the apparently never-ending to-do list, team conversations, emails, and meetings. Particularly when you want to dedicate some time to the things that are most important to you, most of us can't afford to become digital hermits, so we need practical ways to stay focused in a world that is meant to divert us. Time blocking can help with that.

Let's clarify what time blocking is! One time management strategy is time blocking, which involves breaking up your days into specific time slots. Furthermore, time blocking is setting up certain periods of time for all of your desired activities, not simply meetings and appointments. Your everyday tasks, routines, email catch-ups, errands, relationships, and whatever else you find time for are all included in this.

Therefore, you actually organise and use time for everything that you need to do, predicting how long you anticipate each activity would take rather than haphazardly navigating your days without a strategy. The outcome is a week that is realistically scheduled and has lots of time for concentrating on your top priorities.

The idea behind time blocking is to set aside a certain amount of time for each task and rank your tasks according to significance. It is based on the idea that time is a limited resource that needs to be spent carefully. By making deliberate decisions about how to spend your time and being purposeful with every task, you can stay out of the trap of being busy yet unproductive.

Time blocking your calendar has the advantage of being incredibly adaptable and customisable to your personal preferences. To ensure that you have at least a few hours each day for productive work around your meetings, you can be extremely dedicated and establish a work plan for the full week, draw it out at the start of each day, or begin by setting out placeholder focus time blocks.

The Advantages of Blocking Time

There are many advantages to time blocking that can greatly increase your output and general well-being. First, it facilitates efficient job management by offering a defined framework and avoiding task accumulation. You can prevent being overwhelmed and increase efficiency by dividing your day into small chunks and concentrating on one task at a time. Time blocking also improves your capacity to set priorities and set aside time for crucial activities. It enables you to recognise and cut out time-wasting tasks, which boosts output and helps you reach your objectives.

Additionally, time blocking might help you become more accurate in your time estimation and management. You may more efficiently arrange your day by assigning precise time periods for tasks, which helps you better grasp how long each activity takes. This can result in a more balanced and manageable workload by preventing overcommitment and irrational expectations. Time blocking also promotes present-moment awareness and mindfulness. By allocating specific time to every work, you can completely focus on the here and now, improving focus and decreasing distractions.

Additionally, by making sure that you set aside time for both work-related and personal activities, time blocking helps to maintain a healthy work-life balance. You may prevent burnout and keep up a healthy lifestyle by intentionally scheduling time for hobbies, self-care, and spending time with loved ones. By removing the need to continuously decide what to work on next, time blocking also aids in the reduction of decision fatigue. You may just follow the plan and concentrate on completing things without wasting mental energy on decision-making when you have a set schedule.

Time Blocking Techniques

Conventional time blocking: Setting aside particular times during the day for particular work is the most basic kind of time blocking. For instance, email correspondence is handled between 9 and 10 am. For people new to time and task management, this method is straightforward and a good choice. No specialised time-blocking software is needed!

The Pomodoro technique: Francesco Cirillo developed the Pomodoro technique in the 1980s to reduce procrastination and boost output. The concept is straightforward. One Pomodoro is when you set a timer, work for twenty-five minutes, and then take a five-minute rest. You take a longer pause every time you finish four Pomodoros.

Blocking time in batches: Batching is the practice of combining related jobs into a single block, which improves focus, streamlines labour, and speeds up completion. For instance, you're an SEO expert and must submit monthly reports. You spend two hours doing a batch of reports for all your clients at once rather than working on projects for each one. Instead of changing contexts, you're always working on the same task. This method is perfect for repetitive tasks that often follow the same procedure from beginning to end.

Time theming: Although the block is larger, time theming and blocking are comparable. It means dedicating whole days or portions to working on various themes in your work. Instead of allocating a block to a specific activity, you'll allocate it to a more general category inside the same context.

Time blocking for energy management: Using this method, you design time slots according to your innate energy levels. For instance, you'll set aside time to complete your most critical tasks from 9 to 11 am if you know this is when you are most productive. You'll do the least important things for the day between three and five since your energy levels are at their lowest. This lessens tiredness and helps you design a workflow that works for you. Even though this time-blocking technique works well, it takes time and effort to determine when you're most productive.

Thus, time-blocking is an essential strategy for Muslimah mumpreneurs aiming to maximise their productivity. Allocating specific time slots for various tasks, such as client meetings, administrative work, content creation, and family commitments, ensures a structured approach to daily responsibilities.

Managing Distractions

Working mothers must efficiently manage distractions to preserve productivity, lower stress levels, and attain work-life balance. This will ultimately enable them to successfully fulfil their obligations to their families and their careers. As a stay-at-home mother with children, how do you deal with distractions?

Being a mother is a difficult job; when you combine it with the obligations of raising children and starting your own business, it feels like you're pulling a mountain uphill while wearing a blindfold and holding your hands behind your back. As mothers, we all want to provide our kids the time and care they require, but we must also prioritise our needs and hobbies.

Working mothers frequently deal with distractions, which can originate from various sources. These can include internal distractions like racing thoughts or an excessive emphasis on non-work-related tasks, as well as external ones like noise and interruptions. Children's needs, other family obligations, and house maintenance problems can all be additional sources of distraction.

These interruptions can (and do) have a major negative effect on productivity at work, often leading to heightened stress. Do you know that feeling? Half of your focus is on the children, and you feel bad about not being fully present, while the other half is on work, and you feel like you're failing there, too.

Take a moment. Grab a cup of coffee, and spend fifteen minutes listing all the things that have diverted your attention during the past 24 to 48 hours—just scribble it on any scrap of paper. You might be surprised by what comes up. The good news? There are techniques mompreneurs may employ to control distractions and boost productivity. Let's explore them!

Strategies to Minimise Distractions and Stay Focused

Distractions are inevitable when working from home, but they can be managed with the right strategies. One effective approach is setting specific 'work zones' where distractions are minimised. Keeping the workspace separate from high-traffic areas of the house helps maintain focus.

Selecting a quiet, well-lit area away from high-traffic zones helps minimise distractions while boosting mood and energy levels. Investing in ergonomic furniture, such as a comfortable chair and sturdy desk, promotes good posture and reduces physical strain during long working hours. Personalising the workspace with elements like plants and a suitable colour scheme enhances creativity and makes the area more inviting.

Establishing clear boundaries by communicating work schedules with family members ensures minimal interruptions, helping to maintain focus. Keeping the workspace organised with shelves or filing cabinets reduces stress and improves efficiency, making locating essential documents and tools easier. Setting specific work hours helps delineate professional time from family time, fostering a structured routine. Additionally, defining clear goals and rewarding achievements maintains motivation and provides a sense of accomplishment. By implementing these strategies, mumpreneurs can create a functional, comfortable, and productive work environment tailored to their unique needs.

Practising mindfulness and setting clear intentions before starting work can also enhance focus. Beginning the day with a brief dua and asking Allah (SWT) for barakah (blessings) in one's time and efforts fosters a sense of purpose and clarity. Staying disciplined and motivated requires a strong mindset and a commitment to staying on track with business goals. With intentional effort, discipline, and reliance on Allah's (SWT) guidance, a Muslimah entrepreneur can build a flourishing business while fulfilling her role as a dedicated mother and wife.

Chapter Seven

Time Management Techniques for Busy Mothers

Motherhood is a full-time job on its own, and when combined with the demands of running a business, time can often feel like a scarce resource. In the fast-paced world of entrepreneurship, managing one's time efficiently is more than a luxury; it's an absolute necessity.

For female entrepreneurs, time is incredibly valuable. There are always more things to do and deadlines to fulfil than hours in a day, which is the reality of launching and running a business. As a result, it is critical that you, as a female entrepreneur, recognise the value of time management and maximise each minute to accomplish your objectives.

Achieving a healthy work-life balance has personal advantages in addition to the pragmatic ones associated with time management. For many female entrepreneurs, the distinction between business and personal life can become hazy, resulting in stress, burnout, and other detrimental effects. Therefore, establishing a regimen that encourages both work and relaxation is essential.

Striking a balance between your personal and work lives can be quite difficult. By becoming an expert in time management, you can restore control and find balance in your hectic schedule. Let's examine practical methods that support Muslimah mumpreneurs in realising their greatest potential in their personal and professional lives.

Daily Scheduling and Planning

Time is one of the most valuable blessings given by Allah (SWT), and managing it wisely is essential for both personal and professional success.

> *The Quran emphasises the significance of time in several verses, including: "By time, indeed, mankind is in loss, except for those who have believed and done righteous deeds and advised each other to truth and advised each other to patience." (Quran 103:1-3)*

A structured schedule helps balance responsibilities, reduce stress, and ensure that work and family obligations are met efficiently. Mothers, in particular, play a crucial role in nurturing their families while managing businesses or careers. Planning daily, weekly, and monthly tasks can create harmony between these responsibilities and personal well-being.

Creating Daily, Weekly, and Monthly Schedules

A well-structured plan clarifies tasks and ensures no important duty is overlooked. The Prophet Muhammad (PBUH) was known for his disciplined approach to time management. He divided his day into specific portions, ensuring time for worship, family, and the community. His example teaches us that organising one's day allows for a balanced life without neglecting spiritual, personal, or professional responsibilities. A successful schedule should:

> *The Prophet (PBUH) said, "The most beloved of deeds to Allah are those that are most consistent, even if they are small." (Sahih Bukhari)*

This teaches us that consistently managing daily tasks, whether in work, worship, or family responsibilities, is more effective than sporadic efforts. Life is unpredictable, and Islam encourages adaptability. The Prophet (PBUH) adjusted his plans when needed, demonstrating that while having a structure is crucial, being flexible is equally important.

Islam does not encourage overburdening oneself.

> *The Prophet (PBUH) advised his companion Abdullah ibn Amr, "Your body has a right over you, your eyes have a right over you, and your family has a right over you." (Sahih Bukhari)*

This highlights the need for self-care alongside responsibilities.

Monthly, Weekly, and Daily Planning

Monthly Schedule: Provides a roadmap for long-term planning, including financial goals, major family events, and key deadlines.

Weekly Schedule: Helps break down major tasks into manageable portions, ensuring a steady workflow.

Daily Schedule: Focuses on specific priorities, ensuring that each day is productive while allowing time for prayer, family, and rest.

> The Quran reminds us: "And do not waste (your resources) extravagantly. Indeed, the wasteful are brothers of the devils" (Quran 17:26-27)

This verse teaches the importance of not squandering time—a resource more valuable than wealth. By effectively structuring our time, we honour this divine blessing and follow the example of the Prophet (PBUH), who perfectly balanced worship, work, and family life.

Use of Smart Tools & Efficient Scheduling

A mother's best friend when it comes to maintaining organisation is technology. Make use of automation tools and methods to expedite business procedures and save time. In the modern digital era, many time management tools are available to help female entrepreneurs manage their to-do lists and accomplish their company goals. Task management apps and project management software are two popular options that can help you stay organised and on track. With these tools, create to-do lists, set deadlines, and track the status of tasks.

Using Planners, Apps, and Tools for Efficient Scheduling

Video conferencing is one of the greatest ways to meet with clients in this digital age. Thanks to this technology, conducting online meetings from anywhere in the world is simple with just a few button clicks! Zoom and Google Meet are two of the most popular options available online. You may easily incorporate either option into your calendar booking service (like Calendly or Acuity) or embed it into your calendar invites.

Project management software is excellent for managing your ongoing activities and projects. It can assist you in maintaining organisation and meeting deadlines while monitoring your progress. If you're working on several projects at once or need to work with others to finish a job, this is very crucial. Asana, ClickUp, Trello, and Monday.com are examples of popular tools. Find out which appeals to you the most by doing your own research. While some, like ClickUp, have many applications, others, like Trello, are more straightforward. While this appeals to many, it can be daunting to others.

Social networking has become a very useful tool for companies of all sizes. You can effortlessly manage several social media accounts from a single dashboard using social media management solutions like Later or Plann, all while monitoring data like impressions and interaction rates. This greatly simplifies scheduling posts in advance and tracking their performance once they go live! You may start with something like Airtable to arrange your graphics and material and even put it on a calendar view if you're not ready for a full-fledged social media planning tool.

On the other hand, a physical planner can be a great alternative for those who prefer traditional methods. By integrating these tools into daily life, mothers can better manage their time and reduce the mental burden of remembering everything. There is no denying that launching or expanding a business can be intimidating!

But if you have the correct set of fundamental business tools on hand, such as social media management tools, project management software, video conferencing software, and invoicing software, you'll be ready to tackle any obstacle head-on!

Do your homework and select the right tools for your needs. Additionally, choose tools you'll truly use, take your time and ensure they align with your objectives. Enjoy the process. You'll eventually find a tech stack that suits your demands, and you'll be amazed at how much time you're saving.

Delegating and Outsourcing

As a busy mother and entrepreneur, wearing multiple hats throughout the day is an inevitable part of life. However, knowing when to delegate or outsource tasks is key to staying sane and successful. This is a practice that many entrepreneurs, including mothers, overlook because they feel the need to control every detail of their business. While it's natural to want to handle everything, you must recognise that you cannot do everything yourself. There are only so many hours in a day, and trying to stretch your time thin will eventually lead to burnout and decreased efficiency.

Delegating and outsourcing are powerful tools that can help lighten the load, freeing up more time for what truly matters. The concept of delegating is not new, and even in the time of the Prophet Muhammad (PBUH), he delegated responsibilities to his companions, ensuring that each person was assigned duties that best suited their skills. This practice of delegation reflects a deep understanding that no individual can manage everything alone, and teamwork is necessary for success.

Delegation is the process of entrusting a task or responsibility to someone else. It doesn't mean you're relinquishing control; it means recognising others' skills and expertise to help achieve your business goals. Whether delegating household chores, childcare, or certain business tasks, delegation allows you to focus on higher-priority tasks that need your attention.

Outsourcing takes delegation a step further by hiring external individuals or companies to complete tasks or projects that require specialised skills or take up too much of your time. This could involve hiring a virtual assistant to handle emails and scheduling, employing a social media manager to handle content creation and engagement, or contracting out bookkeeping and accounting tasks. Outsourcing can also include hiring freelancers or agencies for marketing, design, or technical work outside your expertise.

Delegating Household Responsibilities

As a mother, your responsibilities at home can often be overwhelming. Between cooking, cleaning, helping with homework, and managing your family's daily needs, it can feel like there is little time left to work on your business. The first step in creating a balanced schedule is acknowledging that household tasks can be shared.

Start by involving your children in age-appropriate chores. Not only does this lighten your load, but it also teaches your children responsibility and life skills. Even young children can help by setting the table or putting away their toys. Assign them more complex tasks as they grow, such as folding laundry or organising their rooms. It's important to create a routine where everyone in the family plays a part in maintaining the home.

Consider hiring help for tasks that require more time and attention. A cleaning service, for example, can take care of deep cleaning once a week, allowing you to focus on your business or personal time. If hiring a full-time helper isn't feasible, look into scheduling part-time help for household cleaning or grocery shopping. Many local services offer flexible options that fit different budgets.

Outsourcing Business Tasks

When running a business, countless tasks require attention but may not necessarily require your direct involvement. Outsourcing these tasks can free up valuable time that you can use to focus on growing your business or spending time with your family.

One of the first areas to consider outsourcing is customer service. Many entrepreneurs spend hours answering emails or handling customer inquiries. However, some services can provide virtual assistants to manage your customer support, allowing you to focus on more strategic aspects of your business.

Social media management is another area where outsourcing can make a significant difference. Social media platforms are essential for modern businesses, but managing them can be time-consuming. By hiring a social media manager or utilising scheduling tools like Buffer or Hootsuite, you can ensure that your posts are consistent without spending hours each week curating content and responding to messages.

If your business involves accounting or financial management, outsourcing these tasks can save you a great deal of time and stress. Hiring a professional accountant or using accounting software to automate invoicing, expense tracking, and tax filing allows you to avoid spending hours on spreadsheets and financial statements.

Trusting the Process

Delegation and outsourcing require trust, which can be a difficult barrier for many women, especially mothers. It can be challenging to let go of control and trust others with responsibilities that may feel personal. However, trusting others to handle certain tasks is a sign of strength, not weakness. It's a way to ensure that you're prioritising what matters most—whether that's your family, your health, or the growth of your business.

It's important to set clear expectations when delegating or outsourcing tasks. Be specific about your needs, desired outcomes, and deadlines. Communication is key to ensuring that the person or team you've delegated to understands exactly what you require.

Additionally, follow up regularly to monitor progress, but give them the space to complete tasks independently. This approach fosters mutual respect and ensures the work is done according to your standards without micromanaging.

The Power of Letting Go

Letting go of the need to do everything yourself is not just about creating more time—it's about improving your mental health and well-being. Many mothers experience stress and guilt when they try to juggle everything independently. This pressure can lead to feelings of inadequacy and frustration. Learning to let go and rely on others doesn't mean you're failing; you're managing your resources effectively to achieve your goals.

Remember that time is a finite resource as you continue to grow your business and manage your personal life. There's no shame in asking for help, whether that's from a family member, a business partner, or a professional. By delegating household responsibilities and outsourcing business tasks, you lighten your load and empower others to contribute to your success.

Time management is essential for any entrepreneur, but it's especially crucial for mothers balancing family life with the demands of business ownership. Delegating and outsourcing are strategies that can help you make the most of your time, allowing you to focus on your priorities without sacrificing the success of your business or the well-being of your family.

Remember that you don't have to do everything on your own—by trusting others with tasks and embracing delegation, you can build a more balanced and fulfilling life as a mother and entrepreneur.

Chapter Eight

Self-Care and Personal Well-being

Maintaining a healthy work-life balance requires looking after your mental and physical health. Setting self-care as a top priority is more crucial than ever, particularly in today's hustle culture. We're continuously faced with new demands and assignments and frequently develop an obsession with efficiency. Perfectionism can easily take over and cause you to put a lot of pressure on yourself.

Meetings, networking gatherings, making decisions, and other duties are all part of running a business. It's simple to overlook your most valuable resource while you strive for achievement and expand your company: yourself! Prioritising your health and well-being is perfectly acceptable. Self-care is essential; it's not a luxury.

What causes us to overlook this crucial area of our lives? When we're first starting out as mumpreneurs, we're eager to see results. There is a phrase in German, "higher, schneller, weiter", which means "faster, higher, further". Because we evaluate ourselves against seasoned business owners, that is what we aspire to in life. There are success tales everywhere we look. We're prepared to put in as many hours as necessary and do whatever it takes to make a sale tomorrow because we want to see results quickly. We also neglect to look after ourselves.

The unpredictable nature of our lives as entrepreneurs, particularly in the beginning, is another major reason self-care is ineffective or frequently neglected. No matter how much you plan and organise, you may receive requests for meetings or invitations to intriguing events interrupting your days. Our work becomes chaotic, and we overlook our own needs due to this uncertainty. We have several half-finished projects, and we believe we can multitask and attempt to progress in many different areas simultaneously. This context-switching affects productivity by raising stress levels and causing weariness.

Self-care is more than simply a trendy term or idea. It encompasses all you do to preserve or enhance your mental, emotional, and physical health. It's about making the conscious decision to care for yourself rather than waiting until you're exhausted or ill. You can choose what works best for you regarding self-care, ranging from journaling and meditation to exercise and a nutritious diet. In the end, self-care is about prioritising your health in your daily life and realising how important it is to your company's success.

Self-care in Islam is essential for maintaining physical, mental, and spiritual well-being.

> *The Quran encourages balance in life: "And do not forget your share of the world, and do good as Allah has done good to you" (Quran 28:77)*

> *The Prophet Muhammad (PBUH) emphasised self-care, saying: "Your body has a right over you" (Sahih Bukhari)*

Caring for oneself strengthens the ability to worship and serve others. Islam promotes proper nutrition, rest, and emotional well-being.

The Prophet (PBUH) also advised moderation: "The best of deeds are those done consistently, even if small" (Sahih Bukhari)

There are a number of strategies for practising self-care and putting your mental health and general well-being first. Being ambitious and working towards your objectives is vital, but it's also critical to do it in a healthy way.

Prioritising Self-Care

Self-care is often pushed to the bottom of the priority list in the whirlwind of managing a business and a household. However, taking care of oneself is not an indulgence but a necessity. The Prophet Muhammad (PBUH) taught balance in all aspects of life, emphasising that our bodies and minds have rights over us. Ignoring self-care can lead to exhaustion, frustration, and even a decline in overall effectiveness as a mother and entrepreneur.

Importance of Self-Care for Mental and Physical Health

Self-care is essential for maintaining mental clarity, physical health, and emotional stability. Women, especially mothers, are natural nurturers, often prioritising their families and businesses over themselves. However, neglecting self-care can result in burnout, anxiety, and even physical ailments.

Self-care is the comprehensive, doable strategy for attending to the physical, mental, spiritual, emotional, and social facets of your life to improve your general health and wellness. We learn early on that we must be strong and put forth much effort. Because to succeed in life, we must put in double or three times as much effort as others. Keep trying. Don't give up. These qualities are commendable.

However, these qualities, combined with our desire "to have it all" or to please everyone, can be a burden if they cause us to prioritise our demands over our own. Since fostering self-care involves doing what makes you feel good, the ideas behind it usually differ from person to person. The first step is regaining energy and taking time for self-care when you feel exhausted and burned out.

It's no secret that working women take on various roles, from managing houses to moving up the corporate ladder. Although this strength and flexibility are commendable, they can also have a negative impact on mental health. As a working woman, you must take care of your mental health. By putting your health and well-being first, you're making sure you have the emotional stamina to handle the demands of life and your family. Making minor adjustments to enhance your well-being is easy. Avoid starting off with unattainable goals. Treat others and yourself with kindness.

Let's make a few things clear. Although self-love and self-care are sometimes confused, they are not the same thing. Self-love is the profound respect and admiration for oneself, whereas self-care is the act of taking steps to maintain or enhance one's health. It's your mindset that initially enables you to take care of yourself. Consider self-love as the attitude that says, "Hey, you deserve that nap!" and self-care as the good deeds you do for yourself, such as taking a well-earned nap. Both are necessary and being aware of the differences enables you to approach each with clarity and purpose.

Engaging in regular self-care helps maintain patience, reduce stress, and improve decision-making skills. When a woman takes care of herself, she is better equipped to handle responsibilities and enjoy the journey of motherhood and entrepreneurship.

Practical Self-Care Routines and Practices

It's critical to comprehend how important it is to incorporate self-care into daily activities, particularly for working women. Let's examine useful self-care techniques that may be incorporated into even the busiest schedules, emphasising mental and physical well-being. Finding time for self-care may seem impossible, but even small, consistent habits can make a significant difference. A few practical self-care practices include:

Conscientious Morning Hours:

Spend a few minutes practising mindfulness to start your day. Before the day's hectic activities start, spend five minutes meditating, deep breathing, or expressing thankfulness. This is an easy approach to centring yourself and can help you establish a positive tone for the remainder of the day. Even basic software, like Insight Timer, can be used.

Following morning Fajr prayer, engaging in dhikr (remembering Allah SWT) can be a potent self-care exercise that promotes serenity, thankfulness, and a spiritual bond as the day begins. Because we're caring for a bounty that Allah (SWT) has bestowed upon us, remember that taking care of you is an act of worship. We not only fulfil our religious duties but also fortify our bodily and mental well-being when we treat our body and mind as holy trusts.

Establish Mini-Moments of Calm:

Throughout the day, schedule brief, purposeful pauses. These little bursts of relaxation, whether a little stroll or a concentrated breathing technique, can reduce tension and improve concentration. Think of it as a reset button for the body and mind amid hectic scheduling demands.

Eat Healthy Food and Be on Time:

Since food serves as our bodies' fuel, we must feed ourselves wholesome meals. Once more, start small. Replace a sugary snack with a piece of fruit or serve your meal with a side of vegetables. Little adjustments can have a major impact on your mood. Meal planning in advance is a useful strategy to promote healthy eating. Simple, healthful meals prepared ahead of time guarantee that you'll always have a nourishing choice available.

> The Prophet (PBUH) said: "The son of Adam does not fill any vessel worse than his stomach. It is sufficient for the son of Adam to eat what will support his back. But if he must do it (fill his stomach), then one-third for food, one-third for drink, and one-third for air." (Tirmidhi)

Incorporating vegetables, whole grains, and protein-rich foods into daily meals facilitates maintaining a well-rounded diet. Furthermore, vitamins and minerals—found naturally in fruits and vegetables—may also contribute to a healthy lifestyle. A diet high in vibrant plant-based foods can provide these vital components.

Since health is one of Allah Almighty's bounties, we should be attentive to it. We frequently take our health for granted, and when it is lost, we lose everything—including our dreams, our healthy bodies, and even the small daily activities we enjoy.

Digital Detox:

Make time every day to unplug from all electronic gadgets. A 30-minute digital detox can help you sleep better, feel less stressed, and re-establish a distraction-free connection with loved ones. Yes, put those devices away for at least an hour before bed and read a real book (yes, they still print real books).

Introspection:

Set aside some time every day to reflect on yourself. Journaling, thinking about your objectives, or just sitting quietly and reflecting on your day can help you achieve clarity, anxiety reduction, and self-awareness.

Sleep and rest:

Remember, sleep and relaxation are essential elements of self-care. Make getting enough sleep a priority by setting a regular bedtime and furnishing a quiet resting space. A rested body promotes a rested mind, which is essential for general health.

Turn to Allah (SWT):

Women are extremely sensitive creatures, so when things get hard, we frequently feel broken. For instance, the never-ending care for your children or the ongoing housework can occasionally feel too much to handle as a mother. Similarly, as a businesswoman, you could experience depression due to the strain of juggling your work and social obligations.

Speaking with Allah (SWT), who created you and loves you more than your own mother, is the finest approach to dealing with such feelings. He is more aware of our circumstances and conditions than we are. This passage from the Quran is sufficient to make us at peace:

> *"And indeed, we have created humankind, and we know what their souls whisper to them, and we are closer to them than their jugular vein"* (Quran 50:16)

Allah (SWT) addresses His people directly in the Quran, and reading it will bring you serenity. Remember to offer five prayers each day! Every prayer is a great chance to be closer to Allah (SWT), reflect on your day, and release any tension or anxieties you may be holding. Beyond being a ceremony, prayer offers numerous practical and spiritual advantages.

Taking Care of Your Mind to Become Resilient:

For Muslim mothers, self-care strategies are essential for mental health. Journaling about thankfulness and introspection within a religious context are examples of practices that can effectively express emotions and foster spiritual development. Learning from Islamic texts or lectures also serves as a kind of mental self-care, strengthening faith and enhancing the intellect. These self-care strategies are essential for developing emotional fortitude and resilience.

Look for Positive Spaces and Knowledge:

Continue to learn about wellness and health from an Islamic and medical standpoint. Look into books, blogs, podcasts, and videos that offer advice on leading a balanced and active lifestyle. Be in a helpful environment with people who will support and encourage you as you work to improve your health and well-being.

Overall, for many of us, focusing on staying active and leading a balanced lifestyle is a lifelong journey. However, we may accomplish this aim and improve our physical, mental, emotional, and spiritual well-being by making tiny daily progress. This will enable us to complete our Muslim obligations and give back to our communities.

Engage in Meditation Practice:

During one of his frequent retreats to the cave of Hira for meditation and solitude, the Prophet (PBUH) heard the first revelation from Allah (SWT). We can find fulfilment via meditation, just as Jesus did when he was alone. It's an effective method of fostering your mental and spiritual well.

Dhikr (remembering Allah SWT) and dua are two ways to meditate. It facilitates a closer relationship between you and Allah (SWT). These duas will help you remain patient if you're having a tough time.

As the Quran beautifully states: "Surely in the remembrance of Allah do hearts find comfort" (Quran 13:28)

Try allocating a little period of time each day to concentrate on your breathing, consider your blessings, or recite passages from the Quran to include meditation into your daily routine. A brief silence can provide a sense of calm; it doesn't have to be long.

Social Networks:

Take care of your relationships. Social ties are essential to mental well-being. Make it a point to communicate with friends and family regularly, even if it's only by text or phone call. These relationships can provide a feeling of community, humour, and support. Think about going on a retreat getaway where you can meet other women who share your interests and undergo a complete reset.

Schedule Self Care:

Remember to include self-care time on your calendar like a doctor's appointment. You're more likely to complete your self-care tasks if you treat it as a priority. Scheduling self-care can also help establish a routine, making it simpler to include in your everyday schedule. Review your regimen regularly.

What's effective? What isn't? Make any necessary adjustments. Recall that there is no one-size-fits-all approach to self-care. What suits one individual may not suit another. Consistency is essential in every regimen. As mentioned, just like you would with any essential appointment, schedule your self-care activities. Build your regimen gradually, starting small. If done regularly, even ten minutes of meditation or a quick stroll might have a significant impact.

It's critical to remember that self-care is not about perfection. It's acceptable if your routine doesn't go as planned on some days. The aim is overall wellness, not perfection. Establishing a self-care regimen is an individual process. The most important things are finding what works for you and staying with it. When you take care of yourself, you can better handle life's obstacles and provide for others.

As Muslims, we consider life to be full of challenges. Choose your response even though you can't choose which tests you take. Everybody experiences hardships in life; some people suffer less than others, while others endure more than we do. When going through difficult times, we lose sight of the blessings Allah (SWT) has already given us. Therefore, instead of whining about what we lack, we should be thankful for what we have.

> *"And He has granted you all that you asked Him for. If you tried to count Allah's blessings, you would never be able to number them. Indeed humankind is truly unfair, (totally) ungrateful." (Quran 14:34)*

Thus, self-care can be practised in various ways. The greatest kind is a regimen that feels fun and manageable. Small, sustainable decisions made daily help women feel their best without contributing to their stress levels by making self-care a simple and organic aspect of life.

Muslim women can adopt a comprehensive approach to spiritual wellness by incorporating self-care into their regular acts of worship and mindfulness. Being a working woman gives you the chance to set an example. Demonstrate that you can prioritise yourself and still achieve professional success.

Managing Stress and Avoiding Burnout

Running a business while raising a family is a rewarding yet demanding journey, and it is crucial to recognise signs of stress before they escalate into burnout. Understanding how to manage stress effectively ensures that both personal and professional responsibilities are handled with clarity and composure.

Identifying Signs of Stress and Burnout

Burnout is not an immediate occurrence but a gradual process that develops over time. It often begins subtly, with minor signs that may be easy to dismiss. However, as stress accumulates, the symptoms become more pronounced, affecting both mental and physical well-being. One of the earliest indicators is persistent fatigue. This goes beyond normal tiredness and persists even after a full night's sleep. No matter how much rest a person gets, they may wake up feeling drained, struggling to find the energy to get through the day.

Physical discomfort is another common sign. Prolonged stress can cause frequent headaches, muscle tension, and body aches. The body remains in a heightened state of alertness, leading to tension-related pain that does not seem to have an obvious cause. These physical symptoms often serve as warning signals that something deeper is at play. Ignoring them can lead to more serious health concerns, including chronic pain and increased vulnerability to illness.

Emotional exhaustion is also a hallmark of burnout. A person experiencing burnout may feel detached, unmotivated, and emotionally depleted. The enthusiasm and passion they once had for their work or personal life may fade, leaving them feeling indifferent or numb. Simple tasks may seem overwhelming, and even small inconveniences can trigger frustration or irritability. This emotional strain can spill over into relationships, causing tension with colleagues, friends, or family members.

Another major consequence of burnout is a decline in productivity. Tasks that were once manageable become difficult to complete. Concentration weakens, decision-making becomes harder, and efficiency drops. A person may find themselves staring at a screen for extended periods, unable to focus, or struggling to keep up with responsibilities that once felt routine. This decline in performance can create a cycle of stress, as the inability to complete tasks leads to further frustration and anxiety.

Over time, burnout can strip away the joy found in previously enjoyable activities. Hobbies, social outings, and even moments of relaxation may no longer bring the same sense of fulfilment. A person might withdraw from activities they once looked forward to, feeling disconnected from their surroundings. This emotional withdrawal can lead to a deeper sense of isolation, making it even harder to recover.

Recognising these symptoms early is crucial. Identifying burnout in its initial stages allows for intervention before it escalates into a severe crisis. Taking proactive steps, such as setting boundaries, prioritising self-care, and seeking support, can prevent burnout from taking a serious toll on both personal well-being and professional success. Addressing the warning signs can help restore balance and create a healthier, more sustainable lifestyle.

Effective Stress Management Techniques and Relaxation Strategies

Islam provides a holistic approach to stress relief. Implementing these techniques can help maintain balance:

- Regular Salah (Prayer): The five daily prayers offer structured moments to pause, connect with Allah, and find solace in His presence.

- Deep Breathing and Dhikr: Practising deep breathing while repeating dhikr (remembrance of Allah SWT) calms the nervous system and refocuses the mind.

- Time Management: Organising tasks using planners or digital tools can reduce feelings of being overwhelmed.

- Seeking Support: Talking to a trusted friend, spouse, or mentor can provide relief and new perspectives.

- Nature Walks: Spending time outdoors and appreciating Allah's (SWT) creation can be a powerful stress reliever.

- Delegation: Learning to delegate tasks at home or for work prevents overload and creates space for personal well-being.

Self-care is not a luxury but a responsibility. When a Muslimah mumpreneur prioritises her well-being, she sets an example for her family and creates a strong foundation for success. By embracing self-care practices, managing stress proactively, and maintaining physical and emotional health, she can navigate her dual roles with grace and strength.

Chapter Nine

Nurturing Relationships and Family Life

A successful Muslimah mumpreneur understands that while business growth is essential, her family remains the cornerstone of her life. Nurturing relationships with her spouse and children, balancing personal and family needs, and effectively handling conflicts and stressors are vital aspects of maintaining a harmonious household.

Let's explore strategies to strengthen family bonds, ensure effective communication, and manage challenges when juggling business and family responsibilities.

Maintaining Strong Family Bonds

Family bonds are the cornerstone of a stable and fulfilling life. A strong family unit provides emotional support, instils values, and nurtures faith. Islam places immense importance on maintaining harmonious family relationships, which are the foundation of a righteous society.

When families are united in love, respect, and mutual understanding, they create an environment where individuals can thrive spiritually, emotionally, and socially.

> The Prophet Muhammad (PBUH) emphasised the significance of family ties, saying: "The person who severs the ties of kinship will not enter Paradise." (Sahih Bukhari and Muslim)

Allah (SWT) also commands believers to uphold the bonds of kinship:

> "And fear Allah, through whom you ask one another, and (do not cut) the wombs (ties of kinship). Indeed, Allah is ever, over you, an Observer." (Quran 4:1)

Strategies for Nurturing Relationships with Your Spouse and Children

A thriving business should never come at the expense of family relationships. For a Muslimah mumpreneur, creating harmony between her entrepreneurial pursuits and her role within the family is vital. The home should be a sanctuary, a place of warmth, love, and mutual respect. This requires conscious and consistent effort, beginning with the marital bond and extending to the relationship with her children.

A strong and loving relationship with one's spouse is the backbone of a nurturing family environment. It sets the home's emotional tone and influences each family member's overall well-being. Allah (SWT) beautifully reminds us of the divine nature of the marital bond in the Quran:

> "And among His signs is that He created for you from among yourselves spouses that you may find tranquillity in them, and He placed between you affection and mercy. Indeed, in that are signs for a people who give thought." (Quran 30:21)

This verse emphasises the elements of tranquillity, affection, and mercy, all essential for maintaining a healthy marital relationship. These qualities don't happen automatically; they're nurtured through intentional acts. One way to do this is by regularly expressing gratitude toward your spouse. Appreciation can uplift the heart and reinforce feelings of being seen and valued. Whether acknowledging your husband's help with the children or his support in your business, those simple words of thanks can go a long way.

The Prophet Muhammad (PBUH) was the perfect model of compassion and kindness in his relationships.

> *He said: "The best of you are those who are best to their wives, and I am the best of you to my wives." (Tirmidhi)*

This hadith sets a high standard of behaviour, emphasising mutual kindness, patience, and gentleness. Prioritising quality time, even amidst busy schedules, is vital. It could be as simple as having tea together after the children are asleep or sharing a walk while discussing your thoughts and dreams. These moments of connection strengthen the emotional intimacy between husband and wife.

Equally important is maintaining open and respectful communication. Disagreements are natural, but how they are handled makes the difference. Approaching discussions with the intention of understanding, not winning, and listening without interrupting creates a safe space for honest conversations. Respecting each other's roles and ambitions helps build a supportive environment where spouses can flourish individually and as a team.

The key to a successful relationship with one's children is presence and engagement. While managing a business can be demanding, carving out time for your children communicates that they matter. Even brief moments of undivided attention—such as listening to their stories, asking about their day, or reading a book together—build trust and emotional closeness.

Children thrive in environments where they feel seen, heard, and loved. The Prophet Muhammad (PBUH) was known for his gentleness with children. He would greet them warmly, carry them on his shoulders, and listen to them with full attention. His behaviour teaches us that kindness and patience are fundamental aspects of parenting.

Incorporating Islamic values into daily life helps children build a strong spiritual identity. Activities like praying together, reading the stories of the Quran, or discussing the names and attributes of Allah (SWT) create an atmosphere of *iman* within the home. These shared spiritual practices educate and strengthen the bond between mother and child.

It is also important to involve children in day-to-day responsibilities. Asking for their help in small tasks makes them feel important and teaches responsibility. Whether it's setting the table, sorting laundry, or helping with meal prep, these interactions also provide opportunities for conversation and learning.

The Quran reminds us of our duties as parents and the importance of valuing our children, regardless of financial fears:

> *"And do not kill your children for fear of poverty. We provide for them and for you. Surely, the killing of them is a great sin."* (Quran 17:31)

This verse underscores the importance of trusting in Allah's (SWT) provision and nurturing our children with love, compassion, and care.

Parenting also means setting limits and guiding behaviour with wisdom. When needed, discipline should be approached with fairness and explained clearly. Children respond better when they understand the reasons behind rules. Avoid harshness or shaming and instead focus on teaching through love and consistency.

For the Muslimah mumpreneur, success in business is a noble pursuit—but true success is found in nurturing the family relationships that Allah (SWT) has entrusted to her. It is a delicate balance, but with intention, dua, and a heart anchored in faith, it can thrive both at home and in entrepreneurship.

Make your home a place of peace and love—where your spouse feels appreciated, your children feel cherished, and the remembrance of Allah (SWT) is ever-present. Through small daily efforts, sincere prayers, and a commitment to your family's well-being, you create a legacy rooted in love, faith, and purpose.

Creating Quality Family Time and Meaningful Interactions

Quality time with family is not just about physical presence but about fostering meaningful interactions that deepen emotional bonds. Intentional efforts to spend time together create lasting memories and strengthen relationships. Whether through planned activities or spontaneous moments, prioritising family engagement ensures a nurturing and supportive environment.

One effective way to enhance family connection is establishing rituals to encourage interaction. Simple traditions, such as a weekly game night, storytelling sessions, or evening walks, offer opportunities for bonding. Engaging in these activities helps children feel valued and heard while reinforcing a sense of belonging. The Prophet Muhammad (PBUH) exemplified the importance of quality time by interacting with his family in ways that made them feel cherished and respected.

Another key element is minimising distractions during family moments. Setting aside devices during meals, conversations, and shared activities fosters deeper engagement. A dinner table free from screens allows for open discussions where family members can share their thoughts, experiences, and concerns. This practice strengthens relationships by encouraging trust and active listening.

A structured yet flexible approach to integrating family time into daily life is essential. Instead of viewing it as an additional responsibility, embedding quality interactions into everyday routines makes sustaining it easier. Cooking meals together, folding laundry as a team, or involving children in grocery shopping transforms routine tasks into bonding experiences. Though seemingly small, these moments contribute to a sense of unity and shared purpose within the household.

Beyond daily activities, faith-centred interactions bring spiritual depth to family relationships.

> *The Quran reminds believers of their responsibility toward their families: "O you who have believed, protect yourselves and your families from a Fire whose fuel is people and stones…" (Quran 66:6)*

This verse underscores the duty of guiding loved ones toward righteousness. One practical way to implement this is by praying together, instilling a sense of discipline and spiritual connection. Encouraging children to recite Quranic verses, discuss Islamic teachings, and reflect on their meanings strengthens their faith while deepening family bonds.

The Prophet Muhammad (PBUH) also encouraged spiritual togetherness within families, stating:

> *"When a man awakens his wife at night, and they pray together, they are recorded among those who remember Allah." (Abu Dawood)*

Engaging in acts of worship as a family nurtures a household environment centred on faith and devotion.

Balancing entrepreneurship with family responsibilities requires mindful time management. A Muslimah mumpreneur should set clear boundaries to ensure work commitments do not overshadow family priorities. Allocating dedicated time for loved ones daily, even if brief, conveys that family remains a top priority. Scheduling special outings or dedicating weekends to uninterrupted family engagement helps maintain this balance.

Equally important is creating an atmosphere of mutual support. Encouraging open conversations where each family member feels comfortable expressing themselves builds emotional security. Validating children's feelings, acknowledging their efforts, and being attentive to their concerns fosters a nurturing relationship. Similarly, showing appreciation for a spouse's contributions strengthens marital harmony.

Family interactions should also be filled with warmth and kindness. The Prophet Muhammad (PBUH) was known for his gentle and affectionate nature. He often played with children and treated them with love. His approach highlights the significance of positive reinforcement and encouragement in parenting. Using kind words, offering praise, and showing patience contribute to a loving and supportive home.

Fostering meaningful interactions can help families build an environment rooted in love, faith, and understanding. Prioritising quality time, strengthening spiritual connections, and maintaining open communication ensure that family relationships remain strong despite life's challenges. When nurtured with care, these bonds become a source of comfort, joy, and unwavering support for all household members.

Balancing Personal and Family Needs

Balancing personal aspirations with family responsibilities is essential for a fulfilling life. A Muslimah mumpreneur must prioritise her well-being to nurture her family effectively. Allocating time for self-care, spiritual growth, and personal development enhances one's ability to support loved ones. Establishing boundaries between work and home life ensures neither is neglected. Seeking Allah's (SWT) guidance, practising gratitude, and maintaining realistic expectations help create harmony between personal and family needs.

Addressing the Needs of Each Family Member While Managing Business Responsibilities

Balancing business and family life requires intentional planning and prioritisation. Every family member has unique needs that must be acknowledged and addressed. A spouse may require emotional support, children may need guidance, and the entrepreneur herself needs time for personal growth and self-care. Setting boundaries and managing time wisely makes it easier to fulfil these responsibilities without feeling overwhelmed.

Flexibility is crucial in achieving balance. A structured daily plan that includes designated work hours, family activities, and personal relaxation time helps maintain stability. Involving children in simple business tasks, where appropriate, allows them to appreciate their mother's work while also spending time together.

Communication and Mutual Support Within the Family

Communication serves as the foundation for a well-functioning family. Transparent and honest conversations about responsibilities, expectations, and challenges foster mutual understanding. When a mumpreneur openly shares her goals and concerns with her spouse and children, they're more likely to support her endeavours.

A supportive home environment thrives on teamwork. Delegating responsibilities, encouraging shared decision-making, and acknowledging each family member's contributions create a sense of unity. Expressing appreciation for each other's efforts strengthens relationships and enhances emotional well-being.

Handling Conflicts and Stressors

Family conflict is a normal but frequently extremely upsetting part of life. Unresolved family conflicts and tensions can affect other facets of life and have a major effect on one's personal health as well as productivity at work. Anxiety, despair, and ongoing stress are just a few of the emotional and mental health problems that can result from ongoing family conflict.

People may experience persistent anxiety, overwhelm, and emotional exhaustion as a result of ongoing tension and unsolved conflicts. In addition to impacting one's well-being, this emotional pressure might make it harder to carry out daily tasks. Emotional discomfort, physical health problems, and decreased productivity are just a few of the negative impacts of family conflict on one's personal life and professional performance. Nevertheless, effective conflict management is achievable with the correct tools and assistance.

Approaches to Resolving Family Conflicts Effectively

Conflict is inevitable in any household, but how it is handled determines the health of relationships. A key principle in Islam is resolving disputes with wisdom and patience. When disagreements arise, maintaining composure, actively listening, and seeking solutions that benefit all parties prevent conflicts from escalating.

A proactive approach involves setting clear expectations and discussing potential areas of concern before conflicts arise. Teaching children conflict resolution skills, such as expressing feelings respectfully and practising forgiveness, fosters a harmonious family environment. Encouraging an atmosphere of kindness and empathy helps prevent misunderstandings from becoming major disputes.

Managing Stress When Balancing Business & Family Life

Running a business while managing a household can be demanding, and stress is unavoidable. However, stress can be managed effectively through strategic planning, delegation, and self-care. Recognising personal limitations and seeking help when necessary prevents burnout.

One essential strategy is setting realistic business goals that align with family commitments. Rather than striving for perfection in all areas, focusing on progress and embracing flexibility allows for a healthier work-life balance. Additionally, incorporating regular self-care practices, such as engaging in hobbies, performing acts of worship, and spending time in nature, enhances emotional resilience.

A supportive network also plays a crucial role in stress management. Seeking guidance from fellow entrepreneurs and family members provides emotional and practical support. Prioritising well-being ensures a mumpreneur can manage challenges with clarity and strength.

A successful Muslimah mumpreneur is not only defined by her business achievements but also by the strength of her relationships and the love within her household. By intentionally nurturing family bonds, balancing personal and professional responsibilities, and effectively managing conflicts and stressors, she creates an environment where both business and family life can flourish. A fulfilling entrepreneurial journey enhances, rather than disrupts, the blessings of family life. With faith, commitment, and thoughtful strategies, a Muslim woman can thrive in both her personal and professional roles, leaving a lasting legacy of love, unity, and success.

Chapter Ten

Leveraging Technology for Efficiency

As a Muslimah mumpreneur, balancing the demands of motherhood and business is both a blessing and a challenge. With the fast-paced nature of today's world, technology has become an invaluable tool in managing both roles effectively. By using it wisely, we can create a sense of harmony between our entrepreneurial pursuits and family responsibilities rather than feeling overwhelmed. From productivity apps to digital organisation and maintaining healthy online boundaries, technology can empower us to streamline our work, stay organised, and grow personally and professionally.

Productivity Tools and Apps

Running a business while nurturing a family requires intentional time management and efficiency. Alhamdulillah, technology has provided us with countless apps and tools that simplify daily tasks, making it easier to handle multiple responsibilities. Whether using a planner app to schedule important meetings, automation tools for business operations, or online learning platforms for self-improvement, the right digital resources can be life-changing. As Muslim women, we recognise the immense value of time.

> *"By time, indeed, mankind is in loss, except for those who have believed and done righteous deeds and advised each other to truth and advised each other to patience." (Quran 103:1-3)*

This verse reminds us to be intentional with our time, ensuring that our efforts—both in business and family life—are aligned with our faith and purpose. By optimising our schedules and leveraging technology mindfully, we can create a workflow that allows us to succeed in both dunya and akhirah.

As a Muslimah mumpreneur, every hour of the day is precious. Balancing business and family requires smart strategies, and leveraging technology can make managing a business more efficient and productive. Alhamdulillah, various apps and tools help streamline different aspects of business operations, allowing us to stay organised and focused.

Task & Project Management

With so many responsibilities, staying on top of tasks is essential. Platforms like Trello and Asana help organise daily work, track progress, and collaborate efficiently. These tools offer visual workflows, checklists, and reminders, ensuring that no important task is overlooked. Simplifying project management allows us to delegate, prioritise, and work smarter.

Note-Taking & Idea Management

A successful business thrives on creativity and planning. Apps like Evernote and Notion provide a structured way to capture ideas, manage schedules, and plan projects—all in one place. Whether jotting down business strategies, brainstorming new product ideas, or organising content plans, these tools help keep our thoughts structured and easily accessible.

Financial Management

Managing finances can be overwhelming, but tools like QuickBooks and Wave make bookkeeping easier by tracking expenses, invoices, and financial reports. By maintaining financial clarity, we can make informed decisions and ensure our businesses grow sustainably. Keeping finances in order also aligns with the Islamic principle of accountability in wealth management.

Marketing & Branding

Strong branding is key to a successful business, and Canva makes professional design accessible to all. Whether for social media posts, flyers, business cards, or logos, Canva provides easy-to-use templates to create visually appealing content without advanced graphic design skills.

Automation for Efficiency

Time is valuable, and automation helps us focus on what truly matters. Zapier connects different apps and automates repetitive tasks, reducing manual work and improving efficiency. By setting up automated workflows, we free up time to concentrate on strategy, growth, and family.

> The Prophet emphasised the importance of excellence in work: "Verily, Allah loves that when anyone of you does something, he does it with excellence." (Sahih Muslim)

By utilising these tools, we can approach our entrepreneurial journey with ihsan (excellence), ensuring productivity while maintaining balance. May Allah (SWT) grant us barakah in our efforts and success in both dunya and akhirah. Ameen.

Achieving a Work-Life Balance through Technology

One of the greatest challenges for mumpreneurs is maintaining a balance between work and family life. The Prophet (PBUH) provided an excellent example of balancing responsibilities. He managed state affairs, guided the community, and attended to his family with care.

> *He also taught: "Your body has a right over you, your eyes have a right over you, and your spouse has a right over you." (Sahih Bukhari)*

This hadith underscores the importance of maintaining a well-rounded life, including self-care, family time, and work. Productivity apps can assist in achieving this balance by helping mumpreneurs allocate time effectively for each aspect of life.

Embracing technology as a mumpreneur is not just about increasing efficiency; it is about being mindful of time, working with excellence, and creating a balanced lifestyle. By utilising productivity tools and apps, mumpreneurs can streamline business operations, manage their time better, and maintain a healthy work-life balance. As Islam teaches us, the wise use of time leads to success in this world and the Hereafter.

> *"And those who, when they spend, do so not excessively or sparingly but are ever, between that, just" (Quran 25:67)*

Just as moderation is key in spending, it is also essential in managing time and responsibilities. By making informed choices using productivity tools, mumpreneurs can build thriving businesses while fulfilling their family roles with excellence and dedication.

Online Resources for Mothers

The internet is a treasure trove of resources designed to support and educate women who balance business and family life. From online communities to virtual learning opportunities, these resources provide both emotional and professional support.

Finding Online Resources and Communities for Support and Learning

Entrepreneurship can sometimes feel isolating, but online communities bridge that gap by providing a support network. Platforms like Facebook Groups, LinkedIn groups, and forums such as Muslimah Entrepreneurs create spaces where mothers can exchange advice, share experiences, and seek encouragement. Virtual networking events and discussion forums allow like-minded women to connect, collaborate, and find mentors to guide them through challenges.

Additionally, websites like Muslimah Bloggers and Mumpreneur communities offer guidance on digital marketing, business strategies, and personal growth. By engaging with these platforms, Muslim women can find solidarity, motivation, and inspiration from others who share similar goals and values.

Leveraging Online Courses and Webinars for Professional Development

Continuous learning is vital for staying competitive in the business world. Online courses like Udemy, Coursera, and AlMaghrib Institute provide accessible education in various fields, from business management to Islamic studies. Webinars hosted by successful entrepreneurs and industry experts offer real-world insights into business growth, marketing strategies, and financial planning. For Muslimah mumpreneurs looking to enhance their skills, these resources are a flexible way to acquire knowledge while managing household and business responsibilities.

Balancing Digital Boundaries as a Muslimah Mumpreneur

As Muslimah mumpreneurs, technology should serve as a means of efficiency and growth rather than a source of stress and overwhelm. In today's fast-paced digital world, excessive screen time and constant connectivity can lead to burnout, distraction, and a diminished sense of presence with our families.

Striking a healthy balance between work, family, and personal well-being is essential, allowing us to nurture our businesses while preserving our mental, emotional, and spiritual health.

Managing Screen Time and Setting Boundaries Between Work and Personal Life

Without clear boundaries, the lines between work and personal life can blur, leading to exhaustion and decreased barakah in our time. To maintain a structured balance, here are some strategies we can implement:

Set Specific Work Hours

Dedicated work hours instil discipline and prevent business tasks from encroaching on family time. Tools like Freedom or StayFocus can help limit distractions from unnecessary websites and social media, allowing us to focus better during work.

Create Tech-Free Zones

Designating areas like the dining table and bedrooms as tech-free zones fosters deeper family connections. Mealtimes and bedtime should be sacred moments for bonding—free from emails and notifications. This practice strengthens relationships and aligns with the Islamic value of being fully present in our roles as mothers and wives.

Implement Digital Detox Periods

Scheduling screen-free periods—such as a no-screen policy during weekends, vacations, or even specific hours—helps reset the mind and reduce digital fatigue. These intentional breaks provide more opportunities for ibadah, reflection, and engaging in enriching offline activities.

Communicate Availability Clearly

Setting clear expectations with clients, team members, and business partners helps prevent work from intruding on personal time. Clearly defined response times ensure that work-related stress does not disrupt moments meant for rest and family.

Use Email Auto-Responders and Scheduling Tools

Tools like Calendly and Google Calendar streamline appointment scheduling, reducing unnecessary back-and-forth messages. Email auto-responders during non-working hours reassure clients while allowing us to prioritise our well-being.

Prioritise Face-to-Face Interactions

While digital communication is convenient, it should not replace meaningful, in-person interactions. Engaging in real-life conversations with our spouses, children, and loved ones strengthens relationships and nurtures emotional well-being.

By setting digital boundaries, we create a structured and fulfilling work-life balance that allows us to be present in both our professional and personal spheres while keeping our hearts aligned with Allah's (SWT) guidance.

Ensuring Secure and Ethical Use of Digital Tools

With the increasing reliance on digital platforms, protecting personal and business data has become more important than ever. For Muslimah mumpreneurs, ensuring digital safety while upholding ethical standards is a professional necessity and a spiritual responsibility. A strong digital foundation helps prevent cyber threats, maintain customer trust, and create a business environment rooted in integrity and Islamic values.

Strengthening cybersecurity begins with practical steps like using strong, unique passwords for different accounts and enabling two-factor authentication to reduce the risk of unauthorised access. Cloud storage platforms such as Google Drive and Dropbox offer encrypted storage, but managing access controls and backups securely is essential. Regularly updating security settings and being vigilant about phishing scams also go a long way in safeguarding business and personal information. The Prophet Muhammad (PBUH) taught us to tie our camels and place our trust in Allah (SWT), reminding us to take necessary precautions even while relying on divine protection.

Digital marketing is another area where ethics must guide actions. In the competitive online space, it's tempting to use aggressive or misleading tactics, but trust is built on honesty. Muslimah mumpreneurs should avoid exaggerations and ensure transparency in all customer communications. Respecting user privacy, clearly explaining how data is collected and used, and refraining from sharing or selling personal information is critical to maintaining credibility. By ensuring their marketing practices align with halal principles, business owners reflect the values of sincerity, fairness, and respect taught in Islam.

As mothers, Muslimah entrepreneurs must also safeguard their children's digital well-being. Monitoring children's online activity, limiting screen time, and using parental control apps like Qustodio and Net Nanny help create a safe browsing environment. Encouraging open dialogue about internet safety and teaching children about privacy, cyberbullying, and responsible usage prepares them to navigate the digital world with confidence and caution. Establishing screen-free zones or time blocks can further promote family bonding and mindfulness.

Educating the entire family about online safety fosters a secure and informed household. Conversations about phishing, safe browsing, and ethical content sharing ensure that everyone, including children and elders, understands the importance of digital responsibility. Privacy awareness—especially when it comes to social media—is crucial. Teaching family members to limit personal information shared online helps prevent unnecessary exposure and potential risks.

In the professional realm, Muslimah mumpreneurs must promote ethical digital work environments. This includes encouraging employees or collaborators to respect confidentiality, practice fair dealings, and maintain professionalism online. Upholding honesty in all transactions, maintaining transparency with partners, and honouring contracts and obligations help build a trustworthy business reputation that reflects Islamic teachings.

By integrating strong cybersecurity practices with ethical digital behaviour, Muslimah mumpreneurs can protect their businesses and families while building a meaningful and sustainable online presence. Instead of feeling overwhelmed by digital challenges, they can embrace technology as a tool for growth—guided by faith, ethics, and intentionality. This balance paves the way for a fulfilling journey in both motherhood and entrepreneurship, rooted in excellence and barakah.

Chapter Eleven

Reflecting and Adjusting Your Balance

Balancing business and motherhood is a continuous journey for Muslimah mumpreneurs. Challenges evolve, circumstances change, and priorities shift. Reflection and adjustment are essential for maintaining equilibrium in both roles.

Taking the time to evaluate your progress, make necessary changes, and celebrate achievements will help you grow both personally and professionally.

Evaluating Your Progress

Setting effective goals involves tracking your progress, as it allows you to prioritise chores and determine how long each task might take. By tracking your progress, you can also determine how to modify your course of action.

Personal development occurs whenever you consciously try to better yourself, whether professionally or personally. Participating in personal development requires you to analyse your growth and the actions you've taken.

Assessing How Well You Are Balancing Business and Motherhood

Balancing the demands of entrepreneurship and motherhood requires ongoing evaluation. It's important to take a step back and ask yourself:

- Am I giving my family the attention they need while maintaining my business effectively?
- Are there moments where one role is overshadowing the other?
- Am I maintaining my mental and physical well-being while juggling responsibilities?

Journaling your daily activities or using productivity tracking apps can help you visualise where your time is going. If you find that your business is consuming more time than planned or that your family responsibilities are taking over your professional goals, it may be time to reassess and adjust.

Reflecting on Achievements and Areas for Improvement

Acknowledging both your successes and areas that need improvement is crucial; look at how far you have come since you started your journey as a Muslimah mumpreneur.

Perhaps you've successfully launched your business, increased your client base, or spent quality time with your children despite a hectic schedule.

At the same time, consider areas where you feel challenged. Do you need better delegation skills? Are you struggling with time management? Do you need to set clearer boundaries? Identifying these aspects will help you make strategic improvements.

Making Adjustments and Setting New Goals

Adapting Your Strategies and Goals As Your Circumstances Change

Life is dynamic, and what worked for you last year may not be effective today. Whether it's a shift in your children's needs, business growth, or personal changes, adapting your strategies ensures you stay aligned with your goals.

For example, if your children have started school, you might find more time to dedicate to business growth. Conversely, if your business has expanded, you may need to establish better routines to maintain balance. Being flexible with your plans allows you to adjust without feeling overwhelmed.

Setting New Personal and Professional Goals for Continued Growth

Goal-setting keeps you motivated and focused. However, your goals should be realistic and adaptable to your changing responsibilities.

For business, consider setting achievable milestones such as launching a new product, increasing sales, or expanding your reach. For personal growth, you may want to set goals related to parenting, health, or self-care.

A useful strategy is to categorise your goals into short-term and long-term objectives. Short-term goals could include setting a structured work schedule or enrolling in an online business course, while long-term goals might involve scaling your business or developing a passive income stream.

Celebrating Achievements and Milestones

Acknowledging and commemorating individual accomplishments is essential for self-improvement. Regardless of their size, these accomplishments are important turning points in our lives. These achievements are worthy of recognition and celebration. These festivities not only give us a feeling of achievement, but they also inspire us to keep going after even bigger objectives.

The whole experience can be improved by giving serious thought to how you commemorate and take advantage of these occasions, whether it's enjoying a delicious treat, spending time with loved ones, or taking a quiet retreat. Your individual preferences and style should be reflected in the celebration.

Additionally, commemorating personal achievements not only benefits us but also serves as a model for others. By publicly recognising and applauding our accomplishments, we encourage people around us to pursue their own goals. Sharing our accomplishments with our friends, family, and coworkers can have a good knock-on impact and inspire others to follow their own aspirations.

Recognising and Celebrating Your Successes in Both Roles

As a mother and an entrepreneur, every small win deserves acknowledgement. Many women tend to downplay their achievements, but celebrating them is essential for motivation. Whether it's successfully managing a difficult week, securing a new client, or creating quality family moments, take a moment to appreciate your efforts.

You can mark achievements with small rewards such as a family outing, personal treats, or a gratitude journal where you document milestones. Acknowledging progress will reinforce your drive to keep moving forward.

Encouraging Continued Motivation and Positive Reinforcement

Success is a journey, not a destination. Staying motivated requires constant self-encouragement. Surround yourself with supportive people who understand your struggles and aspirations. Engage with other Muslimah mumpreneurs, join networking groups, and seek mentorship for continuous learning.

Positive reinforcement doesn't always have to come from external sources. Developing self-affirmations, setting personal challenges, and regularly reviewing progress can help maintain enthusiasm and commitment.

Reflecting on your journey, making necessary adjustments, and celebrating your successes are crucial components of balancing motherhood and business. As you grow and evolve, so will your strategies. By regularly evaluating your progress, setting new goals, and acknowledging achievements, you will continue to thrive as a successful Muslimah mumpreneur. Remember, the journey is not about perfection but maintaining harmony in all aspects of life.

Making Adjustments and Setting New Goals

Life is constantly changing, and the strategies that once worked may no longer be effective. Whether due to evolving family responsibilities, shifting business demands, or personal growth, it's essential to reassess your goals and make necessary adjustments. As a mother and an entrepreneur, being flexible with your plans helps maintain balance and prevents overwhelming feelings.

For instance, if your children have started school, you may find additional time to focus on expanding your business. On the other hand, if your business has grown significantly, you might need to delegate tasks or create a structured schedule to ensure you still dedicate quality time to your family. The key is to remain adaptable, recognise when adjustments are needed, and take proactive steps to realign your priorities.

Parenting and entrepreneurship both require continuous learning and adaptation. As children grow, their needs change, requiring different levels of involvement and care. Likewise, businesses evolve, facing new challenges and opportunities. Recognising when a strategy is ineffective is the first step in making meaningful adjustments.

If you struggle to manage your workload, consider outsourcing minor tasks or automating repetitive processes. Similarly, reassess your work commitments and delegate if family responsibilities become overwhelming. Adjusting strategies does not mean giving up; rather, it ensures that your goals remain achievable and aligned with your evolving circumstances.

Teaching Your Children Business and Financial Literacy

Introducing financial literacy to children from a young age lays the foundation for responsible money management. Teaching them the basics of saving, budgeting, and distinguishing between needs and wants can instil lifelong financial habits. Start by encouraging them to manage their allowances, set savings goals, and understand the effort required to earn money. Simple activities, such as giving them a small weekly budget for personal expenses, can teach valuable lessons in money management. When children learn the value of financial responsibility early on, they grow into adults who make informed and thoughtful financial decisions.

Introducing Entrepreneurship Concepts to Children

Fostering an entrepreneurial mindset in children helps build confidence, independence, and problem-solving skills. Introducing them to entrepreneurship early empowers them to think creatively and take initiative. Encourage them to brainstorm business ideas, create handmade products, or set up a simple business like selling baked goods or offering small services to family and friends. This hands-on approach teaches them business fundamentals, such as planning, customer interaction, and financial management. Entrepreneurship equips children with practical skills and nurtures resilience, innovation, and self-reliance.

Incorporating Islamic Values in Teaching Business Skills

When teaching financial and business concepts to children, incorporating Islamic values ensures they grow up with a strong ethical foundation. Islamic teachings emphasise honesty, integrity, and fairness in financial dealings. By instilling these principles early on, children learn to view success in terms of financial gain and alignment with moral and spiritual well-being. Teach them about halal earnings, the importance of charity (Zakat), and the ethical way of conducting transactions. These lessons help children develop a business mindset that is profitable, socially responsible, and aligned with Islamic teachings.

Practical Activities for Children to Learn Financial Responsibility

Children learn best through experience. Engaging them in practical financial activities can help reinforce the concepts of money management and financial responsibility. Consider allowing them to run a small home-based store, participate in grocery shopping with a set budget, or save for a desired toy or gadget. These activities provide real-world exposure to financial decision-making, helping them understand the value of money, the importance of planning, and the consequences of spending choices. The more hands-on experience they gain, the better prepared they will be to manage finances responsibly as they grow.

Instilling Confidence and Leadership in Your Children

Confidence and leadership skills are crucial for both personal and professional success. Encouraging your children to take initiative and lead in small ways can help develop these qualities. Assign them age-appropriate responsibilities, involve them in decision-making processes, and support their efforts in independent projects. For example, if they start a small business, allow them to handle customer interactions, pricing, and budgeting with guidance. Leadership skills instilled in childhood build the foundation for resilience, adaptability, and problem-solving—essential qualities for future entrepreneurs and business leaders.

By regularly evaluating your strategies, setting new goals, and incorporating financial and business education into your children's upbringing, you create a well-rounded and balanced approach to both motherhood and entrepreneurship. Adjusting to changes with flexibility and fostering leadership in your children will ensure long-term success, both in family life and business.

Reflecting on your journey as a Muslimah mumpreneur is essential for maintaining a balance between business and motherhood. Life is constantly evolving, and adjustments are necessary to align with new circumstances. Regular self-assessment allows you to measure progress, identify areas for improvement, and celebrate achievements. Whether tracking productivity, reassessing time management, or setting new goals, continuous reflection ensures steady growth.

Balancing motherhood and entrepreneurship requires flexibility. If family demands increase, adjusting work commitments can prevent burnout. If business growth demands more attention, restructuring daily routines may help maintain harmony. Small changes, such as delegating tasks or automating processes, can significantly ease the workload.

Equally important is celebrating accomplishments, both big and small. Acknowledging milestones fosters motivation and inspires continued effort. Whether through personal rewards, sharing successes with loved ones, or engaging with supportive communities, recognising progress encourages resilience.

Additionally, instilling financial literacy and entrepreneurial values in children fosters independence and responsibility. Teaching them budgeting, goal-setting, and ethical business principles ensures they develop strong financial habits. By continuously evaluating your path, embracing change, and nurturing future leaders, you create a fulfilling, well-balanced journey as a Muslimah mumpreneur. Success is not about perfection but about growth and harmony.

Building Resilience and Confidence as a Muslimah Entrepreneur

The journey of entrepreneurship is filled with challenges, and for a Muslimah entrepreneur, it often involves unique hurdles and opportunities. From societal expectations to balancing faith and business, building resilience and confidence is key to overcoming these obstacles. For Muslim women entrepreneurs, navigating through these challenges requires a deep sense of inner strength and a supportive network to lean on.

Muslim women entrepreneurs often face cultural expectations or societal limitations, but these challenges can be overcome. Historical examples, such as Khadijah (RA), the first wife of Prophet Muhammad (PBUH), who was a successful merchant, remind us that Muslim women have always been capable of thriving in business. One of the biggest challenges Muslimah entrepreneurs face is the misconception that women, especially Muslim women, cannot be successful in business. By excelling in their ventures, Muslim women can challenge these stereotypes and show the world that entrepreneurship is open to all, regardless of gender or background.

Establishing a network of like-minded individuals is crucial. Connecting with other Muslimah entrepreneurs, whether locally or online, can provide emotional and professional support. This network can also offer mentorship, help navigate challenges, and share resources to assist in business growth. Knowledge is empowering, and Muslimah entrepreneurs should continuously invest in their education and skills development. The more informed and skilled you are in business strategy, financial planning, and marketing, the more confidently you can lead your business.

For a Muslimah entrepreneur, aligning business practices with Islamic values is integral to the journey. Successful entrepreneurship should never compromise faith; instead, it can serve as an opportunity to demonstrate the beauty of Islam through business practices. Conducting business with honesty, transparency, and ethical practices is essential in Islam. Trustworthiness is highly valued in Islam, and running a business with these principles not only leads to success but also brings spiritual rewards. Balancing business commitments with religious obligations like prayers is crucial. With proper time management, a Muslimah entrepreneur can fulfil both her professional and spiritual duties. Creating a daily schedule with prayer times, business tasks, and personal development will keep you grounded and focused.

Seeking Allah's (SWT) guidance is important when making significant decisions. Dua (supplication) and Istikhara (prayer for guidance) can offer clarity and peace of mind, ensuring decisions are aligned with your faith and purpose. Criticism and rejection are inevitable in entrepreneurship, but resilience is built through how you handle them. As a Muslimah entrepreneur, the key is not to let negativity or setbacks define your path. Not all criticism is harmful. Learn to differentiate between constructive feedback and mere negativity. Embrace feedback that helps you improve, whether related to your business model, customer service, or marketing strategy. Use it as a tool for growth, not as a roadblock.

While some criticism is helpful, much of it will be unproductive or even unfair. Focus on your mission and the positive impact your business is making. Tune out negativity and surround yourself with people who inspire and motivate you to move forward. Remember that rejection is a part of the entrepreneurial journey. Every successful entrepreneur has faced setbacks. The key is to not take rejection personally. Instead, view it as an opportunity to learn, grow, and improve.

Building inner strength will allow you to bounce back from difficulties and confidently pursue your goals.

One of the best ways to build resilience and confidence is by learning from those before you. Islamic role models, particularly those successful in their businesses, can provide valuable insights and inspiration. The lives of Muslim women, such as Khadijah (RA), offer rich lessons on entrepreneurship, integrity, and resilience. By studying their journeys, you can draw strength and inspiration to overcome your challenges as an entrepreneur. While modern business environments are different, the core principles of trust, honesty, and perseverance remain the same. Applying these principles from Islamic role models will strengthen your confidence and ensure your business aligns with your values.

Seek out mentors who share your values and vision. Experienced Muslimah entrepreneurs can offer practical advice, provide valuable guidance, and help you navigate the challenges of starting and growing a business.

Chapter Twelve

Conclusion

As you end this book, reflect on the journey you have begun as a Muslimah mumpreneur. This journey is not about reaching a final destination; it is about continuous growth, learning, and striving for balance in every aspect of your life. You have started on a path that challenges you but rewards you, allowing you to honour your faith, nurture your family, and build a meaningful business that aligns with your values. This journey is uniquely yours, shaped by your aspirations and the impact you wish to make on the world around you.

You're more than an entrepreneur and a mother. You are a visionary, a role model, and a leader in your own right. The ability to juggle these roles may seem daunting sometimes, but it is not about perfection. It is about adaptability and perseverance. There will be days when everything flows effortlessly, your business is thriving, and your family is flourishing. On other days, obstacles will arise, and challenges may feel overwhelming. Yet, through it all, with reliance on Allah (SWT) and a steady heart, you will find the strength to navigate those moments. Every difficulty you face is an opportunity for growth, and every success you achieve is a testament to your dedication and faith.

Motherhood and entrepreneurship are not opposing forces. In fact, they complement each other in ways you may not always realise. The skills you develop as a mother—time management, problem-solving, and emotional intelligence—are the very skills that will help you build and sustain a successful business.

Likewise, the discipline and strategic thinking you nurture as a businesswoman will make you a more effective, mindful parent. Both roles require you to give your best, serve with sincerity, and balance priorities in a way that honours your family and professional life. These are not separate spheres; they are interconnected, each enhancing the other and providing you with the tools to succeed.

One of the most powerful aspects of your journey as a Muslimah mumpreneur are your intentions. Your success is not measured by profits or worldly recognition, but by the sincerity of your intentions and the barakah (blessings) that Allah (SWT) places in your efforts.

By keeping Allah (SWT) at the centre of your work, you ensure that your journey is not only fulfilling but sustainable. Ask yourself regularly: Why am I doing this? How does my business serve your family, community, and faith? When your work aligns with your values and the greater good, the rewards—both seen and unseen—are far greater than any worldly measure could offer.

Tawakkul, or reliance on Allah (SWT), is another key component of your journey. This reliance is not about waiting passively for success; it is about doing your best in every situation, making informed decisions, and trusting Allah (SWT) will guide you toward what is best for you. Setbacks and challenges are an inevitable part of any journey, but when viewed through the lens of tawakkul, they are not failures—they are opportunities for growth, learning, and refinement. Every obstacle you face is a divine redirection, a chance to adjust your approach, build resilience, and develop a deeper connection with your faith.

Your work as a Muslimah mumpreneur goes beyond the goal of financial independence. It's about leaving a legacy that impacts not only your own family but also your community and future generations. The business you build today can serve as a foundation for the future, providing not just for your children but also setting an example for other Muslim women to follow. You show that pursuing your dreams, building a successful business, and remaining true to your faith and family values is possible. This is a legacy of empowerment and faith.

True success is not only about what you achieve but about how you uplift others along the way. Whether through mentorship, community involvement, or ethical business practices, you have the power to create a ripple effect of positive change. Imagine the impact you can make on the lives of others by remaining committed to your purpose and striving to do good. By staying true to your values and being a woman of integrity, you are sowing seeds that will blossom into a better future, not just for your family but for the greater community.

As you progress in your journey, continue to set new goals, refine your strategies, and seek knowledge. Surround yourself with a community of like-minded women who understand your challenges and will support you as you continue to grow. Lean on your family for support and guidance, and never forget to turn to the Quran and Sunnah for wisdom and direction. Above all, never stop believing in yourself. You have the strength, the wisdom, and the perseverance to overcome any challenge that comes your way. Trust in Allah's (SWT) plan for you, and know you can achieve great things.

Celebrate every milestone along the way, no matter how small. Every step forward is progress, and every effort gets you closer to achieving your goals. Be patient with yourself and acknowledge your hard work and dedication. This journey is not about perfection but about growth. You are worthy of success, both in this world and the next, and you are more than capable of achieving everything you set your mind to.

Your story is still unfolding, and the best chapters are yet to come. As you step forward with faith, courage, and determination, know you are building something extraordinary. The world needs more empowered Muslim women—women who honour their faith, persevere through challenges, and forge their paths.

Keep striving, and trust Allah (SWT) has already written success in your journey. With every step you take, you are creating a legacy that will inspire generations to come, which is truly extraordinary.

Find Out More

Website: www.barakahinbusiness.com

Socials: @barakahinbusiness

If you enjoyed this book, kindly leave a review to help expand our reach so others may benefit also.

www.ingramcontent.com/pod-product-compliance
Lightning Source LLC
Chambersburg PA
CBHW071213070526
44584CB00019B/3016